The Art of
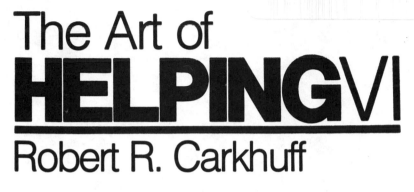
HELPINGVI
Robert R. Carkhuff

SIXTH EDITION

Copyright © 1987 by
Human Resource Development Press, Inc.
22 Amherst Road, Amherst, Massachusetts 01002
413-253-3488

Bernice R. Carkhuff, Publisher

Sixth Edition
Second Printing, August, 1987

Library of Congress Cataloging in Publication Data

International Standard Book No. 0-87425-085-4

Illustrations by Krawczyk
Design by Dorothy Fall
Composition by The Magazine Group
Printing and Binding by Bookcrafters, Inc.

ABOUT THE AUTHOR

Dr. Robert R. Carkhuff is the most-referenced counseling psychologist according to Division 17, American Psychological Association. He is Chairman, Carkhuff Institute of Human Technology, a non-profit institute dedicated to the development and implementation of human resource development, training and performance programs in home, school, work and community settings.

The American Institute for Scientific Information ranks Dr. Carkhuff as the second youngest of the 100 most-cited social scientists, including such historical figures as Dewey, Freud and Marx. He is also author of three of the 100 most-referenced texts, including his two-volume classic, *Helping and Human Relations*.

Dr. Carkhuff is known as the originator of models in helping and human resource development. In his recent work, he has emphasized the human processing—individual thinking and interpersonal processing—essential for human resource development and human performance. His most recent books on human processing are *Human Processing and Human Productivity* and *Learning and Thinking in the Age of Information*.

PREFACE

The Age of Information is upon us. It means constant changes in all areas of living, learning and working. It means a growing need for people with skills. It means a growing need for skilled helpers.

Based upon the most extensive body of research available, The Art of Helping VI *presents an interpersonal skills-based helping model: helpers who offer high levels of interpersonal processing skills will have helpees who demonstrate significantly greater benefits than helpers who offer low levels of interpersonal processing skills.*

The Art of Helping VI *begins by tracing the evolution of helping. It then presents a functional helping model, describing the contributions of both the helpee and helper. The body of the book teaches observable and measurable helping skills. Finally,* Helping VI *points to the future of helping. It culminates with a look at the future growth and development of helpers. It offers the skills we need to be effective helpers in the Age of Information.*

A Personal Introduction

In 1960, as a clinical intern, I saw my first client. I had completed my counseling and therapeutic courses. I knew a lot about the theory and practice of helping. But I did not know what to do.

I asked more experienced practitioners. Their answers varied, depending upon their orientations. One thing they all agreed upon, though, was that the helper had to attempt to understand the client. Yet, not one of them could tell me how to do it.

They offered little help in communicating understanding to a client. One orientation provided me with techniques that helped me to involve the client. Another provided techniques to identify the client's deeper meanings. Still another provided techniques for judging and deciding. And one provided techniques for developing and initiating courses of action.

Later, we studied these techniques to determine if there were any common ingredients (Appendix B). We researched and factored the helping process into responsive and initiative activities. We validated the applicability of these activities to helping people with problems of living, learning and working. We developed research to identify and then use the relationship of people's physical, emotional and intellectual functioning to their problems. But, above all, we studied how people really learn. In experiment after experiment we researched how people become involved in the helping process, explore their experience, understand their goals and take action to achieve their goals.

Those same experiments allowed us to identify the skills the helper needs in order to facilitate the client through the helping process. This book describes and teaches those skills.

As we studied the helping process we discovered that helping was not bound by the four walls of a therapist's office, nor by the minutes of a client-hour. Helping occurred whenever there was a responsive and initiative interaction between people. Such interactions always result in a person's growth. We stopped thinking in terms of therapist and client. Instead, we started thinking in terms of helper and helpee, members of the same team whose relationship was oriented entirely to a human being's growth. These are the terms used in this book.

Research Summary

Over a period of two decades we have refined the application of these helping dimensions in a variety of settings and with different populations. We have now summarized over 20 years of research involving people who were recipients of these helping skills. The results were illuminating. With over 160 studies of over 150,000 people, they indicate the efficacy of interpersonal helping skills. (See Appendix B)

The studies of the effects of helpers with high levels of interpersonal skills upon indices of living, learning and working effectiveness are 96% positive. The studies of the direct effects of training helpees in interpersonal skills upon indices of living, learning and working effectiveness are also 96% positive.

This means that our chances of achieving any reasonable positive living, learning or working outcome are about 96% when either helpers or helpees are trained in interpersonal helping skills. In other words, the chances of achieving negative results for any projects involving high levels of interpersonal skills training for either helpers or helpees are random. Conversely, the chances of achieving any human goal without trained helpers or helpees are random.

I initially distilled these skills programs sixteen years ago in the first edition of *The Art of Helping.* Now, six editions, and more than 250,000 readers later, we are presenting *Helping VI.* Our models of helping continue to evolve. Yet the interpersonal core of helping remains the same. Just as our helping practices grow and change, so do we as helpers, teachers and trainers grow and change. As we continue to grow and change in our skills, so will our helpees, students and trainees grow and gain in their daily living, learning and working activities.

I am in particular debt to John R. Cannon, James T. Chapados and Richard M. Pierce for their contributions to previous editions of *Helping.* In addition, I am appreciative of the continuous support and administrative assistance of Bernice Carkhuff, Debbi Anderson, and Don Benoit for *Helping VI.*

March, 1987   R.R.C.
McLean, Virginia

TO THE READER

The *Art of Helping VI* presents the skills of helping in an organized and easy to read format. Each skills chapter orients you with a simple step chart. At the bottom of every page you will find a few important words which serve to help you summarize the information on that page. To help you review, important phrases and examples are displayed in bold print throughout the book.

You are about to read the sixth edition of what has become a classic in interpersonal skills training. Good reading!

TABLE OF CONTENTS

I.
Introduction

We are born with the potential to grow—no more—no less! Those of us who learn to actualize this potential will know lives of untold fullness and excitement. We will develop growth responses that will enable us to go anywhere and do anything. Those of us who do not learn to actualize this potential will know lives of waste and tragedy.

1.
THE EVOLUTION OF HELPING

Although helping relationships of an informal nature have taken place throughout the history of humankind, formal helping approaches originated in the Industrial Age. Along with psychology and the social sciences, the helping approaches were oriented toward dealing with the changing human experience.

For 10,000 years people had passed on traditional agrarian roles from generation to generation. Then suddenly, with the advent of the Industrial Age, the human conditions changed. Moreover, the conditioned role responses that had given stability to society and, indeed, enabled the advancement of civilization no longer worked.

The Changing Human Condition

Work roles evolved from farming and herding to mechanical processing where humans served as extensions of the machines. With these changes, education—formal and informal—was transformed from an essentially spiritual indcctrination to a scientific and technological orientation. Moreover, living conditions changed as people moved from the towns and villages of isolated farming communities to expanding networks of sprawling cities.

CHANGING CONDITIONS IN LIVING, LEARNING AND WORKING

The changes were incessant as new technologies emerged. Old workers were discarded from declining industries while new workers were demanded by emerging industries. Extended families, once the cornerstone of the old order, were torn apart by the mobility requirements of the new age. Schools were increasingly attuned to the changing requirements: people simply had to learn the basic skills involved in running, and being run by, machines. People needed to learn new responses to live, learn and work in the changing environment of the Industrial Age. As a result, the human condition was changed forever. Never again would it enjoy the stability of the traditional roles that had undergirded its security.

CHANGING RESPONSES TO CHANGING CONDITIONS

Along with technologies, entire societies were transported across the sea to the New World. People of different races, ethnic groupings, classes and roles met and mingled and jostled for the first time in human history. New roles and relationships were negotiated as people battled competitively for new opportunities and the skills to take advantage of the opportunities. Some were left behind in the wake of an often crude social system. Many moved ahead, groping their way from the dark and dreary conditions of the lower class to the seemingly bright opportunities of the middle class. Stripped of their former roles, people began to search themselves for the answer to the basic question of human experience: "Who am I?"

THE CHANGING HUMAN EXPERIENCE

Changing Approaches in Helping

Along with changing conditions and an increasing afflu-
ence, people began to examine their changing human
experience. Early treatment approaches facilitated this
examination, though from different orientations. Freud
and the psychoanalysts viewed adult experience in
terms of early childhood experiences. Watson and the
behaviorists viewed adult behavior in terms of early
childhood conditioning. While the paradigms were
similar, the treatment orientations differed greatly.

The analysts and the neo-analysts, client-centered, existential and other treatment approaches which followed
favored the insight approach. They believed that, with
insight, the patients would function more effectively. In
turn, the behaviorists, neo-behaviorists, trait-and-factor
counselors and other treatment approaches which
followed favored action. They believed that, with the
conditioning of new and more effective responses,
and/or the counter-conditioning of old and ineffective
responses, the patients would function more effectively.
The insight and action approaches were unrelated or
exclusive of each other.

INSIGHT / ACTION

INSIGHT OR ACTION

With the evolution of social learning theory and human resource development approaches, practitioners began to realize that they were not as far apart as they had once assumed. Whether they began with human behavior or with insight, the feedback of practice and research moved them toward one another. Systematically developed insights may be followed by programmatically developed actions in order for the client to function most effectively. Similarly, programmatically developed actions may be consolidated with systematically developed insights. Indeed, personal growth and development in life may be seen in this paradigm: insight ⟶ action ⟶ insight ⟶ action (ad infinitum).

INSIGHT ⟷ ACTION

INSIGHT AND ACTION

The Evolution of the Helping Model

Breakthroughs in helping came from data on helping effectiveness. Basically, helping effectiveness could be accounted for by two factors: responding and initiating.

The responding factor involved the helpers entering the helpees' frames of reference and accurately communicating an understanding of the helpees' experiences. The responding factor emphasized such dimensions as helper empathy or sensitivity, respect or warmth, and sometimes concreteness or specificity in focusing the helpees' experiences. The responding factor facilitated the helpees' exploration of their experiences and the development of insight.

HELPER: Responding

               ↓

HELPEES: EXPLORING
               (Insight)

HELPER RESPONDING → HELPEE EXPLORING

In turn, the initiating factor began with filtering the helpees' experiences through the helpers' experiences. Then, perhaps together, helpers and helpees would initiate a course of action to resolve the helpees' problems. The initiative factor emphasized action-oriented helper dimensions: genuineness or authenticity; self disclosure or helper sharing of personal revelations; concreteness or specificity in problem-solving and program development; and, under specifiable conditions, helper confrontations of discrepancies in helpee behaviors. The initiating factor facilitated the helpees' acting on their problems and reaching their goals.

The responding and initiating dimensions worked together to facilitate the movement from insight to action in the helping process.

PHASES OF HELPING

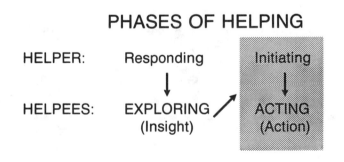

HELPER INITIATING ➞ HELPEE ACTING

Shaped by extensive research and demonstrations in living, learning and working contexts, the helping process was further refined. Personalizing skills serve to facilitate helpee understanding and mediate between helper responding and initiating. The core helping skills facilitated the helpees' movements in intrapersonal processing: exploring where they are in relation to their experience; understanding where they are in relation to where they want or need to be; and acting to get from where they are to where they want or need to be.

PHASES OF HELPING

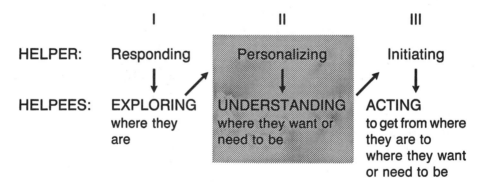

	I	II	III
HELPER:	Responding	Personalizing	Initiating
HELPEES:	EXPLORING where they are	UNDERSTANDING where they want or need to be	ACTING to get from where they are to where they want or need to be

HELPER PERSONALIZING →
HELPEE UNDERSTANDING

The helping model was completed with the pre-helping or attending skills. Attending to the helpees facilitated their involvement in the helping process. The helper engaged the helpees by giving them undivided attention. Helpee involvement triggered helper responding to facilitate exploring. In turn, helpee exploring enabled helper personalizing of helpee understanding. Finally, helpee understanding activated helper initiating to facilitate helpee action.

PHASES OF HELPING

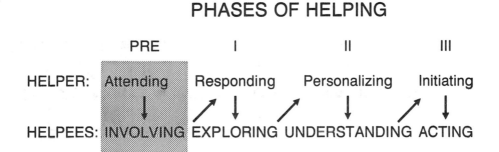

HELPER ATTENDING → HELPEE INVOLVEMENT

Summary

With feedback, the phases of helping are recycled. The helpees receive feedback from acting. The feedback is recycled to stimulate more extensive exploring, more accurate understanding, and more productive acting. The purpose of helping is to engage the helpees in processes leading to human growth and development.

PHASES OF HELPING

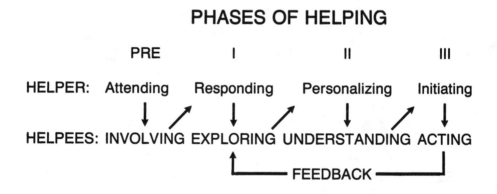

THE HELPING PROCESS

II.
The Helping Process

The sources of helping are the skills and information the participants bring with them. First of all, the helpees bring with them their history of experience and learning. They contribute with their current abilities to process—both cognitively and affectively. Secondly, the helpers bring to helping their own experiences and their processing skills—both cognitive and affective. That is the helpers' contribution to the helping process.

Together, helpers and helpees interact to facilitate their mutual processing—exploring, understanding, acting—of the helpees' problems and goals. That is the essence of helping.

2.
THE HELPEE'S CONTRIBUTION— HELPEE PROCESSING

The Age of Information brings with it extraordinary demands upon human processing. Not only are the information inputs constantly changing, they are also expanding exponentially. This means that many helpees are overwhelmed by the flood of information in their lives. For many, this feeling of being overwhelmed is the very reason that they seek helping in the first place. Within helping, it means that the helpees must process the information that they are unable to process outside of helping. It means that the helpees must have processing skills just as the helpers have processing skills.

The basis of all helping is intrapersonal processing by
the helpees. Intrapersonal processing means looking
within oneself to process personally relevant experiences. Intrapersonal processing involves a basic set of
skills. These skills are familiar to us as the basic skills of
all human processing: exploring human experience;
understanding human goals; and acting upon programs
to achieve the goals. Later on we may learn to teach the
helpees systematic intrapersonal processing skills. For
now, we will learn to facilitate the helpees' movement
through the phases of intrapersonal processing—
exploring, understanding and acting.

PHASES OF INTRAPERSONAL PROCESSING

	I.	II.	III.
HELPEES INTRAPERSONAL PROCESSING SKILLS:	EXPLORING Human Experience	UNDERSTANDING Human Goals	ACTING Upon Programs

FEEDBACK

HELPEE INTRAPERSONAL PROCESSING

Involvement in Processing

Before the helpees can process their experiences, they must be involved. Involvement means that they are prepared for sharing personally relevant experiences. Helpees are prepared for processing by giving their undivided attention.

INVOLVING

HELPEE INVOLVEMENT IN PROCESSING

The helpees prepare to involve themselves by focusing their attention upon their experiences. First, they bring into focus their values or the meanings which they attach to things by looking within themselves. They may begin by asking themselves about their reasons for seeking help. For example, the helpees may have problems in living with their parents or peers. Their values may focus upon handling these difficult situations. That becomes their goal in seeking help. The helpees begin involvement in processing by focusing upon some particular area of living, learning or working.

HELPEE INVOLVEMENT BY FOCUSING

Exploring Human Experiences

Involvement leads to exploring human experience. Intra-personally, exploring means that the helpees are looking within themselves in order to determine where they are in relation to their experiences. They are focusing with their "inner eyes" down and in to exhaust the "nooks and crannies" of their experiences relevant to their helping goals. The helpees explore where they are so that they can understand where they want or need to be.

INVOLVING ⟶ EXPLORING

HELPEE EXPLORING HUMAN EXPERIENCE

We can observe the helpees exploring when they share personally relevant experiences. At high levels of exploring, the helpees share personally relevant experiences with emotional immediacy. At high levels, the helpees also share their experiences with specificity: they detail the experiences they are expressing. The helpees explore themselves by experiencing themselves. For example, a helpee with human relations problems may explore himself or herself as follows:

> "None of my relationships seem to work out—not at home, not at school, not at work. All of the people end up unfriendly. I don't see why I should even try to relate anymore."

The exploration is personally relevant, experienced with immediacy, and expressed with specificity.

HELPEE EXPLORING BY EXPERIENCING

Understanding Human Goals

Exploring human experience leads to understanding
human goals. Intrapersonally, understanding means that
the helpees are searching within themselves for alternative courses of action or responses. They are focusing
their "inner eyes" up and out to generate remedies to
their problems. The helpees attempt to understand
where they want or need to be so that they can act to
get there.

INVOLVING ⟶ EXPLORING ⟶ UNDERSTANDING

HELPEE UNDERSTANDING HUMAN GOALS

We can observe the helpees understanding when they consider alternative courses of action. At high levels of understanding, the helpees have clearly focused goals. This means that they have expanded the courses of action available to them before narrowing to preferred courses of action. They may expand courses by brainstorming or by systematically generating options. They may narrow courses by evaluating them in terms of their personal values and/or the environmental requirements imposed upon them. At high levels of understanding the helpees understand themselves with a high degree of accuracy. For example, a helpee with a human relations problem may understand himself or herself as follows:

> "For my part, I've been messing up. I guess what I have to do is treat them the way I want to be treated. I'd really like to learn to do that."

The understanding is stated with accuracy.

HELPEE UNDERSTANDING WITH ACCURACY

Acting Upon Programs

In turn, understanding human goals leads to acting upon programs to achieve the goals. Acting means that the helpees are planning and implementing action steps. The helpees are focusing their "outer eyes" and selves upon living effectively in their real-life contexts. The helpees act to get from where they are to where they want or need to be.

INVOLVING ⟶ EXPLORING ⟶ UNDERSTANDING ⟶ ACTING

HELPEE ACTING UPON PROGRAMS

We can observe the helpees acting when they design and take action steps to achieve their goals. Acting involves defining specific performance objectives, developing detailed programs to achieve those objectives, and implementing the steps of the program. In this manner, the helpees act programmatically. For example, a helpee with a human relations problem may express his or her acting as follows:

> "I'm going to relate by trying to understand others from their own frames of reference. I'll try to pay attention and be empathic. Maybe then they'll try to treat me in the same way."

The acting is programmatic.

HELPEE ACTING PROGRAMMATICALLY

Feedbacking Information

Intrapersonal processing is incomplete until feedback from acting is recycled. The feedback information is received as input. It serves to generate more extensive exploring of human experience, more accurate under-standing of human goals, and more productive acting upon human programs.

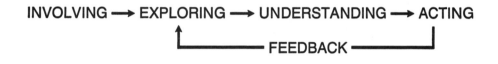

INVOLVING → EXPLORING → UNDERSTANDING → ACTING
                    ⌐————————— FEEDBACK —————————⌐

HELPEE FEEDBACKING INFORMATION

The feedback should be relevant to the helping goal. That is to say, the feedback should provide us information on the helpees' levels of performance. For example, the performance feedback of the helpee with human relations problems may be captured in the following statement:

"The helpee paid attention to, and responded with empathy to his/her parents/peers, and they began to respond in the same way."

This feedback provides information relevant to the original helping goal.

HELPEE FEEDBACKING RELEVANT INFORMATION

Summary

Helping serves to facilitate intrapersonal processing—
exploring, understanding, and acting. Later on, even in
the absence of the helpers, the helpees will continue to
recycle this process throughout their lives. This recycling
of processing in growing spirals is the source of continued growth and development.

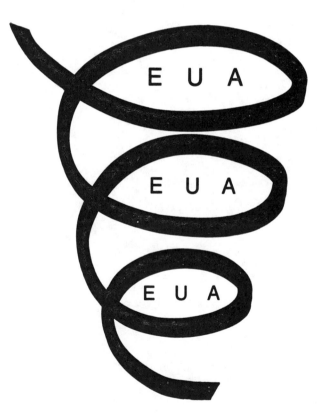

HELPEE INTRAPERSONAL PROCESSING ⟶
HELPEE GROWTH

3.
THE HELPER'S CONTRIBUTION—
HELPING SKILLS

The basic tenet of the Age of Information is interdependency. This means that we are each dependent upon the other in this "global village" which we call Earth. Parents are dependent upon children, teachers upon learners, managers upon employees just as well as vice versa. In this context, the basic helping skills in the Age of Information remain the interpersonal processing skills. They enable one person to relate to the experiences of others. They facilitate the intrapersonal processing of others.

The helpers' interpersonal processing skills serve to facilitate intrapersonal processing by the helpees. Interpersonal processing skills are based upon seeing the world through the helpees' eyes, responding accurately to that experience, personalizing the problems and goals involved, and initiating a course of action to resolve the problems and achieve the goals. Attending skills involve the helpees in helping. Responding skills facilitate exploring by the helpees. Personalizing skills facilitate understanding by the helpees. Initiating skills stimulate acting by the helpees. The feedback from acting recycles the phases of processing. The helpers' interpersonal processing skills facilitate the helpees' intrapersonal processing.

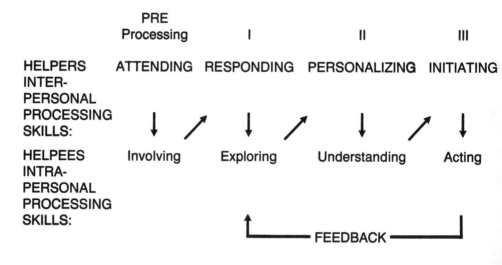

PHASES OF PROCESSING

	PRE Processing	I	II	III
HELPERS INTER-PERSONAL PROCESSING SKILLS:	ATTENDING	RESPONDING	PERSONALIZING	INITIATING
HELPEES INTRA-PERSONAL PROCESSING SKILLS:	Involving	Exploring	Understanding	Acting

FEEDBACK

HELPER INTERPERSONAL PROCESSING SKILLS

Attending to Involve

During the pre-processing stage, the helpers attend to
the helpees in order to involve them in the helping process. Attending involves communicating a hovering or
undivided attentiveness to the helpees. Attending serves
to focus the helpers' observing and listening skills upon
the helpees' verbal and behavioral expressions of their
experiences. These attending skills focus helping upon
the helpees' experiences. Attending also serves to communicate an intense interest in the experiences of the
helpees and so motivates them to get involved in the
helping process.

ATTENDING

↓

Involving

HELPER ATTENDING → HELPEE INVOLVEMENT

The basic attending skills, then, are attending physically, observing and listening. Helpers attend physically so that they can observe. In turn, they observe so that they can listen. Attending physically emphasizes facing, squaring, leaning toward, and making eye contact with the helpees. Observing emphasizes viewing the appearance and behavior of the helpees. Listening emphasizes "hearing" the content and affect of the helpees' expressions of their experiences.

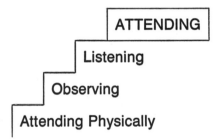

HELPER ATTENDING—ATTENDING PHYSICALLY, OBSERVING AND LISTENING

Responding to Facilitate Exploring

During the initial phase of the helping process, the helpers respond to the helpees' experiences to facilitate the helpees' exploring. The helpers attempt to communicate accurately their discriminations of those experiences. Accurate responsiveness will serve to facilitate or stimulate the further exploration of the helpees' experiences.

RESPONDING

↓

Exploring

HELPER RESPONDING → HELPEE EXPLORING

The helpers respond to the content of the expressions by reflecting what the helpees are saying or talking about. The helpers respond to the affect involved by reflecting how the helpees feel about what they are saying. Finally, the helpers may put the feeling and content together in a response which reflects the meaning of the experiences for the helpees. For example, the helpers may respond to a helpee with problems in human relations as follows:

"You feel alone and hopeless because others always end up rejecting you."

If accurate, this response will facilitate further exploration of experience by the helpee.

| RESPONDING |
| Respond to Meaning |
| Respond to Feeling |
| Respond to Content |

HELPER RESPONDING—TO CONTENT, FEELING AND MEANING

Personalizing Understanding

During the transitional phase of the helping process, the helpers personalize the helpees' understanding of their goals. The helpers attempt to consider the implications of the helpees' experiences for the helpees. Another word for personalizing is internalizing. The helpers make an effort to facilitate the helpees' taking responsibillity for their experiences. Personalizing enables the helpees to transform their problems into goals.

PERSONALIZING
↓
Understanding

HELPER PERSONALIZING ⟶
HELPEE UNDERSTANDING

The helper personalizes the meaning of the helpees' experiences by communicating the direct implications of these experiences for the helpees. The helpees internalize the responsibility or "ownership" of the problems when the helper personalizes the problems for them. When the helper personalizes the goals, the helpees then internalize the responsibility for achieving these goals. For example, the helper may personalize the helpees' understanding of problems in human relations as follows:

> "You feel disappointed because you cannot manage your interpersonal relations with others and you're really eager to learn to do so."

If accurate, this personalized response will facilitate the helpee's understanding of the problem and goal.

PERSONALIZING

Personalize Goals

Personalize Problems

Personalize Meaning

HELPER PERSONALIZING—
MEANING, PROBLEMS AND GOALS

Initating Acting

During the culminating phase of the helping process, the helpers initiate to develop programs upon which the helpees can act. The helpers attempt to define the goals which have been personalized. Further, they attempt to develop programs to achieve these goals. Finally, the helpees implement the programs by acting to resolve their problems and achieve their goals. Initiating by the helpers enables the helpees to act upon their programs.

INITIATING

↓

Acting

HELPER INITIATING → HELPEE ACTING

The helpers begin to initiate by defining the goals with the helpees. The helpers continue to initiate in the development of action programs by defining objectives and developing the tasks and steps needed to achieve these objectives. The next step in initiating is designing schedules and determining reinforcements. The helpers then prepare the helpees to implement the programs and provide feedback with check steps along the way. For example, the helpers may initiate to facilitate helpee acting to achieve human relations goals as follows:

"Your objective is to respond accurately to others' experiences. Your tasks involve attending physically, observing, listening and responding. Your first step is to face the other person."

If appropriate, this initiative program will facilitate the helpee's acting to achieve goals.

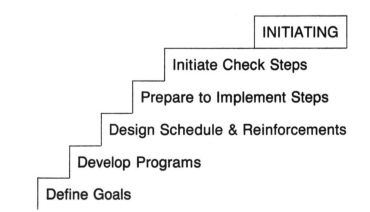

INITIATING

Initiate Check Steps

Prepare to Implement Steps

Design Schedule & Reinforcements

Develop Programs

Define Goals

HELPER INITIATING—GOALS, PROGRAMS, SCHEDULES, REINFORCEMENTS, IMPLEMENTATION AND CHECK STEPS

Facilitating Feedback

Finally, the helpers will facilitate feedbacking information. The emphasis of feedback is upon the effectiveness of the helpees' action responses. If the helpees are
satisfied with their action responses, then they may conclude this area of helping. If the helpees are not
satisfied, then they may recycle processing.

FEEBACKING

↓

Recycling

HELPER FEEDBACKING → HELPEE RECYCLING

The helpers gather performance information then communicate this information to the helpees. The purpose of communicating this information is to tell the helpees how well they performed their responses. For example, the helpees with human relations problems may receive feedback concerning their attempts to respond to the experience of others as follows:

"Your interpersonal responses were (were not) accurate reflections of the experiences of others."

This information feedback allows the helpee to compare response performance with the goal of managing interpersonal relations.

FEEDBACK

Communicate Performance Information

Gather Performance Information

PROVIDING PERFORMANCE INFORMATION

Summary

Interpersonal helping skills (ARPI) enable the helpers to relate to the helpees' frames of reference and engage them in intrapersonal processing (EUA), leading to their growth and development. Later on, the helpers will want to teach the helpees the same interpersonal processing skills so the helpees can guide their own effectiveness in life. In an interdependent, changing world everyone will need both interpersonal and intrapersonal processing skills in order to survive, learn, and grow.

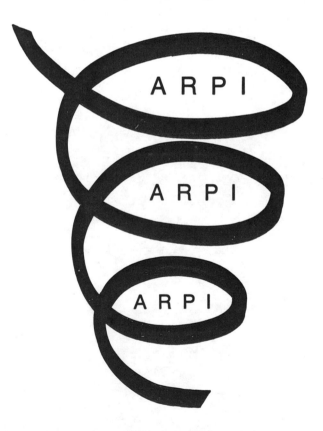

HELPER INTERPERSONAL PROCESSING →
HELPEE GROWTH

III.
Helping Skills

The first year of human development serves as a prototype for all human learning. Initially, the children explore and identify the nature of specific stimuli and responses. Transitionally, the children come to understand the interactive nature of stimuli and responses, anticipate the effect of one upon the other and develop goals to achieve these effects. Finally, the children act by drawing from their developing repertoire of responses to attempt to achieve their goals. The children's behavior is shaped by the feedback, achieved in the environment. This feedback recycles the stages or phases of learning as children explore more extensively, understand more accurately and act more effectively. This ascending, enlarging spiral of exploring, understanding and acting is the source of adults' improving repertoire of responses.

4.
ATTENDING—
INVOLVING THE HELPEE

Our task as helpers is to facilitate the helpees' movements through the phases of learning, exploring, understanding and acting. We begin by involving the helpees in the helping process. We accomplish this by attending to helpees. This chapter will focus on the skill of attending.

Here are some questions that you can ask as you begin to think about attending:

How do you know when someone is really interested in you?

How do you know when someone is being attentive toward you?

What can you learn about people by looking at them?

How do you know when someone is really listening to you?

Read this case study and see if you find instances when the helper is not involving the helpee.

Case Study #1—Nonattending

Katherine is a 20-year-old college student. She has called Joyce, an acquaintance, "to get together and talk." Katherine wants Joyce's advice. Joyce is twenty-one years old and just finishing a Bachelor of Arts in Psychology.

Joyce was not sure why Katherine called her. They were certainly not friends. Joyce doubted if Katherine ever had a close friend. Katherine exasperated people. Joyce and her friends had talked about it several times. No one was sure why Katherine affected people this way. She seemed nice enough, but something about her irritated people.

Joyce was regretting her appointment with Katherine. She really hadn't wanted to see her. On top of that, everything that could go wrong had gone wrong that day. The weather was hot and humid. The bus broke down on the way home so she had to walk the last two miles. Her air conditioner was broken and she didn't have time for a bath before Katherine would arrive. All she could think of was how tired and hungry she was and how badly she did not want to see Katherine. As Joyce was thinking this very thought, the doorbell rang.

Joyce: (distractedly) "Hi, Katherine, come on in." (Joyce walks into the bedroom signalling Katherine to follow. Once there, she starts to change. Katherine stands in the doorway, watching.) "I hope your day was better than mine." (Katherine says nothing. After changing clothes, Joyce leads the way into the living room. Katherine sits on the couch. Joyce takes a chair across the coffee table from her. Joyce lights a cigarette with a deep breath, then exhales.) "Now, what did you want to talk about?"

Katherine: "I . . . I'm not sure where to begin. Well, I just can't seem to make friends. Nobody seems to like me. I . . ."

Joyce: "Oh, come on! I'm your friend. Listen, Katherine, I think you're just too sensitive."

Katherine: "I don't know. No one seems to care."

Joyce: "Would I be talking to you if I didn't care?"

Katherine: (hesitantly) "Nooo . . . but . . ."

Joyce: (interrupting) "Maybe the problem is you're too uptight, you know what I mean? You never seem to be able to loosen up."

Katherine: "I don't know, Joyce. I just feel. . .lonely. I hardly ever have a date and when I do they never ask me out again."

Joyce: "Well, maybe if you fixed yourself up a little bit. You know. . .look more available."

Katherine: "I don't know what you mean."

Joyce: "Come on now, Katherine. If you want to get to know someone you have to let him know you're interested. I'm not talking about being cheap."

Katherine: "I don't know."

Joyce: "Come on, Katherine. You said you were lonely. I've got an idea. Let's go dancing tomorrow night. I have a lot going on tonight, but let's go tomorrow. I'll call you tomorrow to set the time and stuff, okay?" (Joyce stands up and heads for the door. Katherine looks at her.) "I wish I could talk some more, Katherine, but I've got to get crackin'."

Katherine: (as she stands up, looking confused) "Oh, sure."

Joyce: (leaning against the door after Katherine has left, muttering in a low voice) "Why do I get talked into these things?"

Attending is the necessary pre-condition of helping. To understand its critical nature, you may turn away from others in your presence. Ask yourself how you communicate interest in the others. More important, how do you learn about or from the others? As you turn gradually toward the others, you will learn about them. You will learn primarily by what you see and what you hear.

Attending skills posture the helper to see and hear the helpees. They involve preparing for attending, attending personally, observing and listening. Attending skills serve to involve the helpees in helping. When the helper is fully attentive, the helpees become fully attentive and engage in the helping process. Attending lays the base for responding to facilitate helpee exploration.

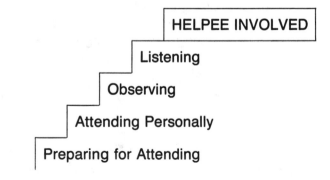

HELPEE INVOLVED

Listening

Observing

Attending Personally

Preparing for Attending

ATTENDING INVOLVES THE HELPEE

Preparing for Attending

The first task in attending is preparing for attending. Like preparation for anything in life, preparing is a necessary but not sufficient condition of involving the helpees. Preparing for attending involves preparing the helpees, the context and the helper. If the helpees are not prepared to make the contact, they will not appear. If the context is not prepared to receive the helpees, they will not return. If the helper is not prepared to attend to the helpees, they will not become involved in the helping process. Preparing for attending prepares us for attending personally to the helpees.

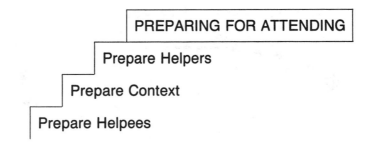

PREPARING FOR ATTENDING

Prepare Helpers

Prepare Context

Prepare Helpees

The helpees' willingness to become involved will depend upon how well we prepare them for the helping interaction. Preparing the helpees involves engaging them, informing them of our availability and encouraging them to use our help.

Engaging the helpees emphasizes greeting them formally and establishing a common frame of reference concerning the purpose of the contact.

Informing the helpees emphasizes communicating:

Who they will be seeing.

When and **where** the appointments will take place.

How to get there.

What the general purpose of the contact will be.

Encouraging the helpees emphasizes providing the helpees with the reasons for becoming involved by answering the following questions:

Why should I get involved?

Why do you want to get involved with me?

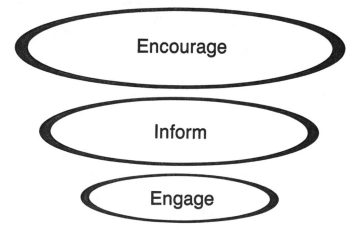

PREPARING THE HELPEES

Our ability to facilitate helpee involvement also depends in part upon preparing the context for the helpee. Preparing the context involves arranging the furniture and decorations and organizing our offices or meeting rooms.

Arranging the furniture emphasizes facilitating open communication by sitting in chairs, facing each other with no desks, tables or other barriers between them. If there are several helpees, the chairs should be placed in a circle to facilitate the communication of interest and attentiveness to one another.

Arranging decorations emphasizes utilizing decorations to which the helpees can relate. For instance, if the helpees are college students, our decorations should reflect things that are familiar and comfortable to them.

Finally, the helping setting needs to be organized in a neat and orderly fashion. That way we communicate that we are on top of our own affairs and ready to focus upon the problems of the helpees.

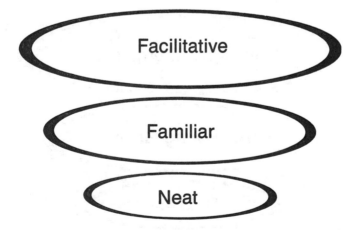

PREPARING THE CONTEXT

It is as important to prepare ourselves for helping as it is to prepare our helpees and the context. We prepare ourselves by reviewing what we know about the helpees and the goal of helping as well as by relaxing ourselves.

Reviewing what we know about helping emphasizes reminding ourselves of what we know about the helpees from all previous interactions. This information may include formal notes, intake data and records as well as informal impressions.

Reviewing the helping goals emphasizes the purpose of the contacts. During the initial stages of helping, the goals will be to involve the helpees in exploring their experiences of their problems.

Relaxing ourselves emphasizes relaxing our minds and bodies prior to the actual helping interactions. Some helpers relax their minds by thinking of pleasant, soothing experiences. Others relax their bodies by physically relaxing one set of muscles after the other. We must experiment and find the method of relaxing that is most effective for us.

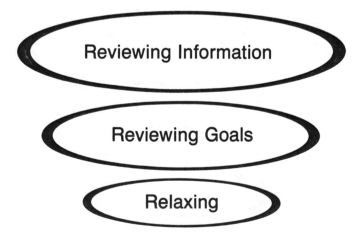

PREPARING OURSELVES FOR HELPING

Attending Personally

By attending personally we bring our helpees into close proximity with us. In so doing, we communicate our interest in the helpees. Communicating an interest in the helpees tends to elicit a reciprocal response of interest from the helpees.

Attending personally involves posturing ourselves to give our full and unidivided attention to the helpees. Attending personally emphasizes facing the helpees fully by squaring with them, leaning forward or toward them and making eye contact with them. Attending personally to the helpees prepares us for observing them fully.

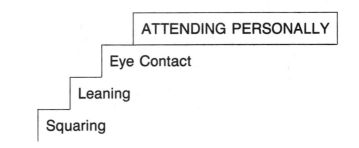

ATTENDING PERSONALLY

Eye Contact

Leaning

Squaring

ATTENDING PERSONALLY

One way of posturing ourselves to attend to the helpees is to face them fully. Whether standing or sitting, we may attend to an individual helpee by facing him or her squarely—our left shoulder to the helpee's right shoulder and vice versa. When we are dealing with a couple or a small group of people, we should place ourselves at the point of a right angle drawn from the people to our extreme left and right. See how differently we feel about the helpees when we posture ourselves in this manner from how we feel when we posture ourselves for purposes of our own comfort.

SQUARING

There are other ways of posturing ourselves to attend personally. The inclination of our bodies is one critical way. For example, when we are sitting we attend most fully when we incline our bodies forward or toward the helpees to a point where we can rest our forearms on our thighs. When standing, we attend most fully when we close the physical distance by moving closer to the helpees. Putting one leg in front of the other will help us to lean slightly toward the helpees.

There are still other ways of attending to people in need of help.

LEANING

We must seek in every way possible to communicate our full and undivided attention. Perhaps the key way of attending personally involves how we use our senses, particularly our eyes. We communicate attentiveness when we maintain eye contact with the helpees. The helpees are aware of our efforts to make contact with them psychologically through our efforts to make contact with them visually.

MAKING EYE CONTACT

We may rate our level of "personal attending while sitting" by using the following scale.

High attending — Squared, eye contact, and leaning 20 degrees or more

Moderate attending — Squared, eye contact

Low attending — Not squared, slouching

LEVELS OF PERSONAL ATTENDING WHILE SITTING

Clearly, we do not always attend personally by sitting. Often we are attempting to help people while standing. We can use a similar scale to rate our demonstration of the skills while standing.

High attending — Squared, eye contact, and leaning 10 degrees

Moderate attending — Squared, eye contact

Low attending — Not squared

LEVELS OF PERSONAL ATTENDING WHILE STANDING

We communicate personal attending by all of our mannerisms and expressions. When we are intense but relaxed, we communicate attentiveness. When we are nervous and fidgety, we communicate a reluctance to be there. When we are consistent in attentive behavior, we communicate interest. When we blush or turn pale, we communicate different levels of reaction to the helpees. It is important to have ourselves "together" in attending behavior.

We can practice our own attending posture, first in front of a mirror and then with people we see in everyday life to whom we want to communicate interest and concern. We may feel awkward at first; after awhile, however, we should notice that we focus more upon the other person and that the other person is more attentive to us.

Perhaps the most important skill that personal attending prepares us for is observing.

**COMMUNICATING INTEREST—
CONSISTENT ATTENTIVE BEHAVIOR**

Observing

Observing skills are the most basic helping skills. They are a rich source of learning about the helpees. When all else fails, we emphasize observing our helpees. We learn much of what we need to know about people by observing them.

Observing skills involve the helper's ability to see and understand the nonverbal behavior of the helpee. We must observe those aspects of the helpee's appearance and behavior which help us to infer the helpee's physical energy level, emotional feeling state, and intellectual readiness for helping. These inferences are the bases for our initial understanding of where the helpee is coming from.

OBSERVING

Infer Energy, Feeling, and Readiness

Observe Appearance and Behavior

OBSERVING

When we observe we collect the nonverbal information
that the helpees present to us. We learn about the
helpees by noting their appearance, specifically their
posture, body build, and grooming. We can also collect
information by observing their behaviors, specifically
their facial expressions and body movements.

From their appearance and behaviors we can make
some inferences about their energy level, feeling state
and readiness for helping.

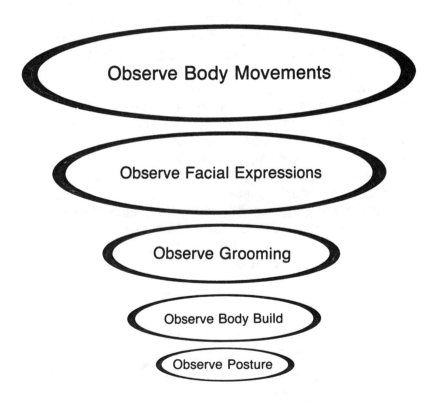

OBSERVING APPEARANCE AND BEHAVIOR

Energy level is the amount of physical effort put into purposeful tasks. Knowing how long people can sustain high levels of functioning is essential to knowing how people experience their lives. Only people with high energy levels can experience the fullness of life. Persons with low energy levels have great difficulty in meeting even the simplest demands of everyday life.

The richest source of information about energy level is communicated by the alertness of the helpee's posture. Specifically, the helper will look for the same cues in the helpee that were discussed earlier in helper attending: the extent to which the helpee stands and sits erect or leans forward with eyes focused on the helper. A helpee who sits slouched with shoulders drooped is taking a position that suggests low energy.

Energy level may also be expressed in body build. For example, helpees who are physically overweight or underweight or have poor muscle tone will tend to have low levels of energy. Cues to the helpees' energy levels can also be observed in grooming and nonverbal expressions. It takes a certain amount of energy to maintain a clean and neat apperarance.

In addition to gathering information from appearance, helpee energy level can be inferred from helpee behavior. For example, slow helpee body movements may infer a low level of energy.

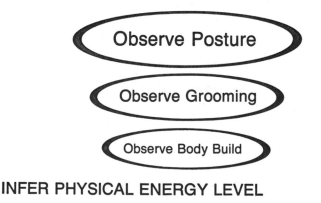

INFER PHYSICAL ENERGY LEVEL

Facial expressions are the richest source of data concerning the helpee's feelings. Other areas, especially posture, also contribute to understanding the helpee's experience. Inferences can also be made based on body movements, with slow movements indicating "down" feelings and overly-swift movements suggesting tension or anxiety. From this data we can infer the helpee's emotional feeling state. For example, a deep furrowed brow, a frown, a slouched posture, downcast eyes, poor grooming, and slow body movements all communicate "down" feelings. A broad smile, raised eyebrows, an attending posture, eye contact, careful grooming and quick responsive body movements are associated with "up" feelings.

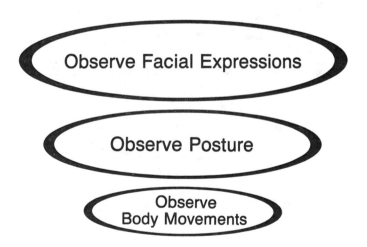

INFER EMOTIONAL FEELING STATE

From our observations of helpee appearance and behavior we may infer a general intellectual readiness for helping. Again, helpee posture is the most powerful cue to readiness for involvement in helping. We can also learn about the helpee's readiness by observing body movements and facial expressions. Relatedly a helpee who has a low energy level and "down" feelings will usually have a low readiness for helping. A helpee with high energy and "up" feelings is usually ready for the helping process.

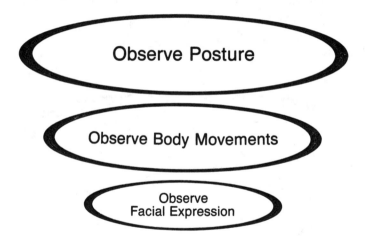

Observe Posture

Observe Body Movements

Observe
Facial Expression

INFER INTELLECTUAL READINESS FOR HELPING

By observing we can gain valuable information about the helpees' experiences. One way of structuring observing is to observe the helpees for precisely the same attending posture which we exhibit as helpers. Based upon our observations of appearance and behavior, we can make inferences about the helpees' functioning. We can infer a helpee's physical energy level, emotional feeling state and intellectual readiness for helping.

It is important to remember that observations must be considered hypotheses to be confirmed or denied over time by the helpee's behavioral and verbal expressions. Observations should not be taken as a valid basis for making snap judgments about a person.

INFERRING FROM OBSERVATIONS

Perhaps one of the most important observations we can make is identifying discrepancies or incongruencies in people's behavior or appearance. Being incongruent simply means that people are not consistent in different aspects of their behavior or appearance. For example, people may say they feel fine while sitting slumped, looking at the floor and fidgeting.

Being incongruent is itself a critical sign of people in trouble. Helpees invariably want to become more positively congruent. Perhaps the most important aspect of behavior to which you can respond initially is the helpees' desire to get themselves "together." More than anything else in the world, the helpees want to be able to function effectively without those glaring inconsistencies in their actions.

OBSERVING INCONGRUENCIES

We can observe ourselves in the same manner that we observe others. What does our appearance and behavior say about us? Do we project a high level of energy, feeling and readiness to help? Are we congruent in our behavior and our expressed desire to help?

We can also use our observations of ourselves and our helpees to involve the helpees. In helping, we should be focusing our entire beings upon the helpees and their expressions of their experiences. In this manner, we are communicating nonverbally that we are attending to them and are focused in our interest in their experiences of themselves. In so doing, we increase the helpees' sense of comfort and security in helping.

OBSERVING OURSELVES

Listening

The sources of input that we most often employ in helping are the verbal expressions of the helpees. What people say and how they say it tells us a lot about how they see themselves and the world around them. Ultimately, the helpees' verbal expressions are the richest source of empathic understanding for the helper.

When we give the helpees our full and undivided attention, we are prepared for listening to their verbal expressions. The more we attend to the external cues presented by the helpees, the more we can listen to the internal cues reflecting their inner experiences. There are many ways that we can develop our listening skills. These include having a reason for listening, suspending our judgment, focusing upon the helpee and the content, and recalling the expression while listening for common themes. Listening prepares us for responding empathically to our helpees.

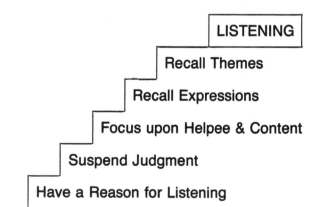

LISTENING

Recall Themes

Recall Expressions

Focus upon Helpee & Content

Suspend Judgment

Have a Reason for Listening

LISTENING

First, as listeners, we should know why we are listening. We should have a reason for listening. The goal of helping is the reason for listening—to gather all of the information that we can related to the problems or goals presented by the helpees.

As with observing, we should listen for cues to the helpees' levels of physical, emotional and intellectual functioning. To do this, we must focus not only upon the words but also upon the tone of voice and the manner of presentation. The words will tell us the intellectual content of the helpees' experiences. The tone of voice will tell us about the helpees' attendant feelings. The manner of presentation will tell us about the helpees' energy levels. For example, content expressed in a dull tone of voice and in a listless manner suggests a depressed helpee with a low level of energy.

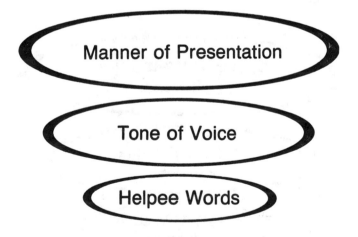

HAVING A REASON FOR LISTENING

Next, it is important to suspend our own personal judgments in listening, at least initially. If we are going to listen to what the helpees say, we must temporarily suspend the things which we say to ourselves. We must let the helpees' messages sink in without trying to make decisions about them.

Suspending judgment means suspending our values and attitudes regarding the content of the helpees' expressions. For example, we may not approve of the helpees' behaviors or the way they are living their lives. However, our feelings are not relevant to the helpees' experiences and our purpose is to facilitate the helpees' growth and development. In addition, we must exercise caution in offering premature solutions, no matter how many times we think we have been over this ground with others. Each helpee has a unique experience, and it is our job to allow the uniqueness of that experience to emerge.

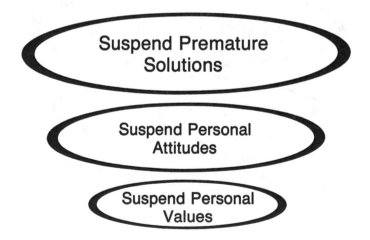

SUSPENDING PERSONAL JUDGMENT

Perhaps the most important thing in listening is to focus upon the helpees. We focus upon the helpees by resisting distractions. Just as we initially resist the judgmental voice within ourselves, so must we also resist outside distractions. There will always be a lot of things going on that will not help us to listen.

We must place ourselves in quiet places so that we can focus upon the helpees' inner experiences. To the degree that we can, we must use a helping context that avoids noises, views and people—anything or anyone that will take our attention away from the helpees to whom we are listening. We must summon all of our energy, affect and intellect to focus upon the helpees' inner experiences and external behaviors so that we can respond accurately to those experiences and behaviors.

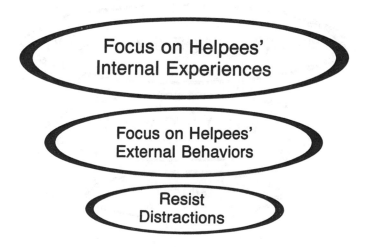

Focus on Helpees'
Internal Experiences

Focus on Helpees'
External Behaviors

Resist
Distractions

FOCUSING UPON THE HELPEES

In listening to the helpees, we focus initially upon the content. In focusing upon the content, we want to be sure that we have all of the details of the helpees' experiences. Otherwise we will not be able to help them to understand their experiences. We focus upon content by asking ourselves the 5WH basic interrogatives:

Who?
What?
Why?
When?
Where?
How?

If we can answer these questions, we can be sure that we have the basic ingredients of the content of the helpees' experiences. If we cannot answer these questions, we should continue to listen. As the helpees share their experiences they will fill in the missing information for us.

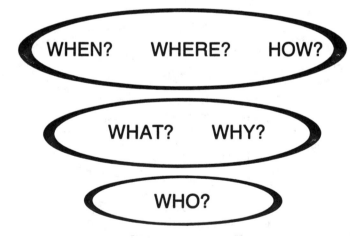

FOCUSING UPON THE CONTENT

We should concentrate intensely enough upon the helpees' expressions to be able to recall both the content and the attendant affect of the helpees. In addition we also want to recall any gaps—missing information.

To practice your listening skills in recalling brief expressions, try to recall the entire expression verbatim. With lengthy expressions, try to recall the gist of it. After you read the following expression of a young man in trouble, try to recall the content, affect and any "gaps" in information.

> "Things are not going so good for me. Not in school. Not with my girl. I just seem to be floundering. I fake it every day but inside I'm really down because I'm not sure of what I want to do or where I want to go."

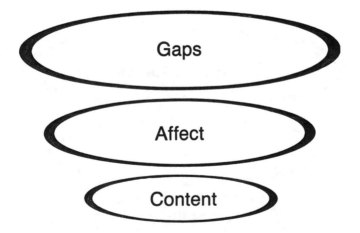

RECALLING THE EXPRESSION

We must also learn to recall the helpees' expressions over a period of time. In so doing, we are looking for the common themes in the helpees' experiences. The helpees' important themes will be repeated over and over. Usually, the helpees will invest the most intensity in these themes because they are trying to communicate them to us.

These themes will tell us what the helpees are really trying to say about themselves and their worlds. They will tell us where they are "coming from" if we just provide them the opportunity. We need only receive the messages they are sending and process them for the common themes. This will prepare us to respond accurately to the helpees.

We should practice listening for themes in our daily conversations. For now, we can use the case studies at the beginning and end of each chapter. See how well we do when compared to the helpers involved.

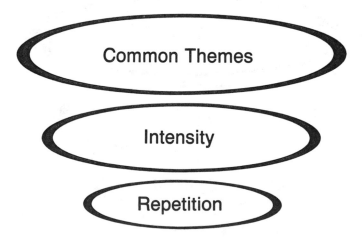

LISTENING FOR THEMES

There is no question that listening is hard work. It requires intense concentration. However, just as there are different rates for reading, so are there also different rates for listening. Most people talk at the rate of 100 to 150 words a minute. Yet we can easily listen at a rate of two or three times that amount. We can put this extra time to use by reflecting upon or thinking about what the helpees have said.

Most of us have been taught not to listen or to hear. Years of conditioning have gone into this. We are distracted because we do not want to hear. We distort the expressions because of the implications of understanding. Most of all, there are the implications for intimacy that make people fearful. Just as we have been conditioned not to listen or hear, now we must train ourselves to actively listen and hear the expressions of the helpees.

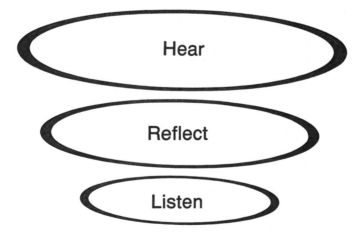

HEARING

Summary

One of the ways of structuring listening is to test our verbatim recall of the helpees' expressions. Simply listen to these expressions and try to repeat verbatim what you heard. We may practice in live interactions or with written or taped expressions. We may rate the accuracy of our recall as follows:

High accuracy — Verbatim recall of expression

Moderate accuracy — Recall of gist of expression

Low accuracy — Little or no recall of expression

In the end, the entire verbal helping process hangs on our ability to listen and process the content and affect of the helpees' expressions.

Now we can begin to build our own cumulative rating scale for helping. If the helper is attending personally, observing and listening to the helpees, we may rate the helper as fully attentive (level 2.0). If the helper is only attending personally, then the helper is rated at a less than fully attentive level (level 1.5). If the helper is not attending personally, then the helper cannot be rated in relation to the helpee (level 1.0).

LEVELS OF HELPING

5.0
4.5
4.0
3.5
3.0
2.5
2.0   Observing and listening
1.5   Attending personally
1.0   Nonattending

LEVELS OF HELPING—ATTENDING

If we have attended to the helpees effectively, then we will have involved them in helping. The helpees will experience comfort in the preparations we made for them. They will experience security in our attentiveness and confidence in our observations. They will begin to share their experiences, and we will have the opportunity to listen and hear their expressions.

Above all else, the helpees will begin to reciprocate by involving themselves in the helping process. They will prepare for their sessions. They will become attentive and observant of themselves and others. They will begin to share their experiences and listen in turn to the expressions of others. In so doing, the helpees will signal their readiness to enter the exploratory phase of helping.

PHASES OF HELPING

PRE

HELPER: Attending

↓

HELPEE: INVOLVING

FACILITATING INVOLVING

Like any other set of skills, you will want to practice the attending skills until you have integrated them into your helping personality as the helper in the following case study has done.

Case Study #2—Skilled Attending

Terry is a 23-year-old male who is tall, broad-shouldered and well-muscled. He appeared to be agitated and angry. When Paula, the therapist, first met Terry it was at her office. Her only preparation was a phone call from a company where she had a contract to provide employee assistance counseling asking her for an emergency appointment for Terry that afternoon.

When Paula walked into the waiting room she was surprised. Terry did not look like her typical client. He was tall, muscular and moved quickly. He wore work clothes, clean but obviously used for their purpose. And he was angry. He was pacing back and forth, his face contorted with the effort of controlling his rage. After hesitating a fraction of a second, she approached.

Paula: (reminding herself to stay relaxed) "Good morning. You must be Mr. Mason."

Terry: "Yeah."

Paula: (extending her hand) "My name is Paula Rantoul." (Terry takes her hand with a grasp which threatens to smash her fingers but turns out to be just a firm handshake.) "Please come into my office. Take the chair by the window; it's the most comfortable." (As Terry sits down Paula offers a cup of coffee which he refuses. Paula sits in a chair opposite Terry, leaning forward.) "Now, I understand you want to see me about some things that are troubling you."

Terry: "---damn right! I just lost my job because I hit my foreman! If I don't learn how to control my temper my whole life will turn to sh--!" (Paula leans forward a little more and looks at Terry frankly.) "I don't know what a little girl like you can do to help me, but I'm ready to give anything a try!"

On he talked for another fifteen minutes, non-stop. Once he jumped up and started pacing, slamming his fist into his hand again and again as he talked. Paula stayed in her chair, turning to face him as he walked back and forth. When he realized what he was doing he smiled sheepishly and sat back down. Finally he stopped his tirade and sitting back in the chair looked at Paula sitting across from him.

Terry: "You know, you got real guts. Most women would have high tailed it out of here or tried to get me to sit still. Why not you?"

Paula: (quietly, looking at Terry) "You don't need another person to be afraid of you nor do you need a mother to criticize you right now. You said you want someone to help you. I've got to find out who you are first if I'm going to be that person. I can't do that if I'm running from you or trying to get you to do what I want."

Terry: (looking baffled for a minute, then smiling) "You really know what you're doing. You'll do."

Paula: (smiling back) "You're too strong to allow me to treat you like a child. You're too strong to allow yourself to act like a child."

Terry: "You know you're right. I don't want to be out of control. All it does is get me into trouble."

It took every one of Paula's attending skills to maintain contact with Terry. She had to attend contextually by preparing herself, the environment and Terry for the interaction. She did that by keeping her tension in control, putting Terry at ease, and by making her office as comfortable and yet as constructive as she could for her interaction with Terry. She made sure she kept good eye contact. She leaned forward and kept herself squared to Terry, even when he was pacing back and forth. She made observations that helped her to recognize that Terry was in control of his anger, but only barely. And she listened to what he was saying, trying to get information for future use.

Her efforts paid off. Her consistent use of attending skills resulted in having Terry commit himself to working with her, recognizing that she could help him grow.

5.
RESPONDING—
FACILITATING EXPLORING

This chapter addresses the skill of responding. We will learn how to respond to the helpees' frames of reference to facilitate the helpees' exploration of their experiences.

Here are some questions that you can ask as you begin to think about responding:

How do you know when you can trust someone?

How do you know when somone has heard you?

How do you know if someone really understands you?

Read this case study and try to identify instances when the helper does not facilitate helpee exploration.

Case Study #3—Unskilled Responding

Matthew Benning is a 76-year-old man who had just been admitted to a nursing home. Up until now he had lived in his own home, a home he built himself fifty years ago. He lived there with his wife, raising four children. His children have all married and have left the area. His wife died two years ago.

Matt had to give up his home after a stroke partially paralyzed his left side. He can talk but needs a wheelchair to get about.

He had been assigned to Carla's floor. Carla is the nursing supervisor for that floor. She has worked at the nursing home ever since she got her R.N. degree six years ago. She tries to be a good nurse and makes sure her staff is "as considerate as possible" of the patients. Following is an excerpt of a conversation between the two of them just after Matt arrived. The conversation took place in Matt's room which he shares with another patient.

Carla: (to Matt's roommate) "Hi Paul. I see you've got a new roommate."

Paul: "Yeah."

Carla: "I'm sure you're going to get along just fine." (to Matt) "Mr. Benning?"
(Matt is lying on the bed, eyes closed. He stirs and opens his eyes.)

Carla: "Mr. Benning, my name is Carla Pope. I'm your nurse. How are you doing?"

Matt: "Huh?" (He sits up on the side of the bed with difficulty because of his left arm and leg.)

Carla: "How are you doing?"

Matt: "Oh fine, fine! Who did you say you were?"

Carla: "My name is Carla. I'm your nurse."

Matt: "Hi, my name is Matt Benning."

Carla: "Yes, I know. May I call you Matt?"

Matt: "Sure."

Carla: "Is there anything you would like?"

Matt: "Uh, no, I don't think so."
(Carla sits on the bed next to Matt.)

Carla: "You're sure?"

Matt: "No, I'm not, but I can't think of anything right now. Say, how long will I have to stay here?"

Carla: "Well that's hard to say. Besides you just got here." (cheerfully) "What's wrong? Don't you like us?"

Matt: "No, no! It's just that I've been away from home for so long. I've got so much to do. I've got to . . . ."

Carla: "Now don't worry about that. I'm sure that everything is just fine. What you need to think about is resting and getting better. Think of this **as** a vacation. Right, Paul?"

Paul: "Huh, what did you say?"

Carla: "Say, have you two met?"

Matt: "No, not yet."

Carla: "Well, since you're going to be roommates. I think you ought to." (cheerfully) "Paul Dobbs, meet Matt Benning."
(Both hesitantly smile and nod to each other.)

Matt: "Hi."

Paul: "Hello."

Carla: "Now, I'm just going to check on dinner and let you two get acquainted. Matt, I'll stop in later to see how you're doing. Pau', you might want to give Matt a cook's tour after dinner. See you later."
(Carla smiles at both, gets up and leaves.)

Responding provides the basis upon which the helping process is built. It facilitates the helpees' exploration of where they are in relation to their worlds. We attend, observe and listen to the helpees so that we can respond to them. Responding emphasizes entering the helpees' frames fo reference and communicating to them what we hear. In other words, there are two separate sets of skills involved: discriminating accurately the dimensions of the helpees' experiences and communicating accurately to the helpees the dimensions we have perceived.

Responding involves responding to content, feeling and meaning. We respond to content in order to clarify the ingredients of the helpees' experiences. We respond to feeling in order to clarify the affect attached to the experience. We respond to meaning in order to provide the reason for the feeling.

Responding facilitates helpee exploring. When the helper responds accurately to the helpees, then the helpees explore where they are in relation to their worlds. Responding both stimulates and reinforces helpee exploring. It lays the base for personalizing to facilitate helpee understanding.

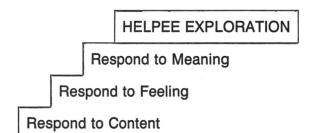

RESPONDING FACILITATES HELPEE EXPLORING

Responding to Content

We respond first to the most obvious part of the helpees' expressions—the content. We respond to content in order to clarify the critical ingredients of the helpees' experiences. Having an accurate content data base enables us to establish our responsive base in helping: responding to feeling and meaning. In turn, the responsive base enables us to personalize understanding and initiate acting.

The ingredients of content emphasize the basic interrogatives which may be summarized as 5WH: who, what, why, when, where and how.

A good response rephrases the helpees' expressions in a fresh way. It does not simply "parrot" back the helpees' own words. A good format for responding to content is:

"You're saying _____."

     or

"In other words, _____."

RESPOND TO CONTENT

Paraphase

Recall 5WH

RESPONDING TO CONTENT

The basic interrogatives provide us with a format for testing the completeness of the helpees' expressions of their experiences. In other words, they enable us to determine whether the helpees have included everything we need to know. The interrogatives may be formulated as follows:

Who and **what** was involved?
What did they do?
Why and how did they do it?
When and **where** did they do it?

For example, in responding to content, we may examine the following expression for the interrogatives:

"I thought I had things together with my teacher."
                                                              WHO?

"But now I flunked the exam."
                                                              WHAT?

"I guess we were on different wavelengths."
"I sure didn't expect questions that hard."
                                                  HOW and WHY?

"I guess I didn't study enough at home before the test."
                                            WHERE and WHEN?

RECALL 5WH

The 5WH helps us to organize details and know if the helpee is leaving things out. The response formulated by the helper however need not repeat the details.

Rather, the helper will *paraphrase* the helpees' content by summarizing it using the helper's own words. A paraphased response to content will capture the main points communicated by the helpee in a brief statement. This will help ensure that the helpee can clearly understand the summary made by the helper.

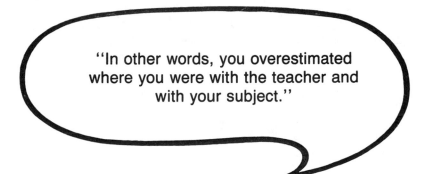

"In other words, you overestimated where you were with the teacher and with your subject."

PARAPHRASE CONTENT

Responding to the content facilitates the helpees' exploration of any "gaps" in the content. If any of the 5WH interrogative questions are unanswered, we may want to probe them to get a more complete picture of the helpees' experiences. However, to encourage helpee exploration we must continue to respond and refrain from asking questions. We will learn more about question asking after we have learned and practiced the skill of responding.

Listen for the 5WH. These essential ingredients will enable us to later diagnose the helpees' deficits. By organizing the content we then communicate our understanding of the content for the helpees. We may wish to practice responding to content in real life or in recorded expressions. Again, the case studies may be helpful material for practicing formulating content responses.

FACILITATING EXPLORING OF CONTENT

Responding to Feeling

Just as we showed our empathy for the helpees by responding to the content of their expressions, we may also show our understanding of their experiences by responding to the feelings which they express. Indeed, responding to content prepares us to respond to the feelings of the helpees' expressions. Responding to feelings is the most critical single skill in helping because it reflects the helpees' affective experience of themselves relative to their worlds.

Helpees may express verbally and directly those feelings which dominate them. Or the helpees may only express their feelings indirectly through their tone of voice or by describing the situation in which they find themselves.

Whether the helpees' expressions are direct or indirect, our goal as helpers will be to explicitly show the helpees our level of understanding of their feelings. This will give the helpees a chance to check out our effectiveness as helpers. It will also give us a chance to check our own level of accuracy.

Responding to feelings involves asking and answering the empathy question and developing interchangeable responses to feelings.

RESPOND TO FEELING

Answer the Empathy Question

Ask the Empathy Question

RESPONDING TO FEELING

To respond to the helpees' feelings, we must do several things. First, as we have learned, we must observe their behaviors. In particular, we must pay attention to the helpees' postural and facial expressions. The helpees' self-expressions will tell us a great deal about how they experience themselves. Their tones of voice and facial expressions will be valuable clues to their inner feelings.

Next, we must listen carefully to the helpees' words. When we have listened to the words, we must summarize what we have seen and heard that indicates the helpees' feelings. Then we ask ourselves the question, "If I were the helpee and I were doing and saying these things, how would I feel?" In answering this question, you can first identify the general feeling category (happy, angry, sad, confused, scared, strong or weak) and the intensity of the feeling (high, medium or low). Then select a feeling word or phrase that fits the feeling area and level of intensity. Finally, check out the feeling expression with your observations to see if it is appropriate for the helpees involved. (For example, it would not be appropriate to use the word "morose" to capture the down feeling of a helpee with a sixth-grade education.)

"How would I feel if I were the helpee?"

ASKING THE EMPATHY QUESTION

By answering the empathy question we try to understand the feelings expressed by our helpee. We summarize the clues to the helpee's feelings and then answer the question "How would I feel if I were Tom and saying these things?"

Tom: "Things are not going so good for me. Not in school. Not with my girl. I just seem to be floundering. I fake it every day but inside I'm really down because I'm not sure of what I want to do or where I want to go."

The main cue to the helpee's feeling is that he says he feels down. He's down about school and down about his relationship with his girl. He's also floundering. If we were in his position, we might very well feel sad.

Practice asking and answering to yourself the "How would I feel?" question with other expressions that you hear in everyday life.

*"I'd feel sad
if I were he!"*

ANSWERING THE EMPATHY QUESTION

We can insure that we respond to the helpees' feelings when we make a response that is interchangeable with the feelings expressed. It certainly is not too much to expect that we be able to communicate to the helpees what they have communicated to us. Understanding what the helpees have expressed—at the level they have expressed it—constitutes the only basis for helping.

A response is interchangeable to feelings if both the helper and the helpee express the same feeling.

The first response which we formulate should involve very simple feeling words reflecting the feelings expressed by the helpee. We may do this by using a simple "You feel _____" formulation. Before we move to more complex communication, we must learn to formulate simple responses.

We may say that we respond to the helpees' feelings when we capture the essence of their feelings in one or more feeling words.

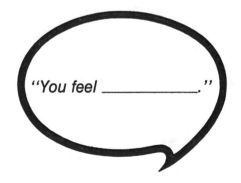

DEVELOPING INTERCHANGEABLE RESPONSES TO FEELINGS

Now let us try to formulate a feeling response to the helpee's expression. Let us repeat Tom's expression again:

"Things are not going so good for me. Not in school. Not with my girl. I just seem to be floundering. I fake it every day but inside I'm really down because I'm not sure of what to do or where I want to go."

Again, we have asked ourselves, "How would I feel if I were he?" We answer, "Sad—I would feel sad." Now we formulate the response in a way that we can communicate directly how he feels: "You feel sad."

"You feel sad."

RESPONDING TO SAD FEELINGS

As you have found, the helpees exhibit many different moods—many different feeling states. Sometimes they seem very sad. Sometimes they seem very happy. Sometimes they seem very angry. Most times they are somewhere in between these extremes.

We must have responses which communicate to them our understanding in each of these moments. We must be able to formulate simple and accurate responses to the helpees' feeling states.

For example, Tom is kind of sad or "down." His energy level appears low. Things seem pretty hopeless. He feels helpless in the face of everything. He just does not know where he is going. Tom verbalizes this feeling when he says, "Sometimes I just think that I'm not going to make it."

Using an appropriate feeling word for this kind of sadness, we might formulate a simple response.

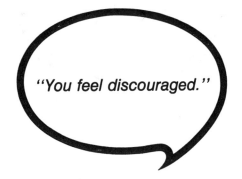

"You feel discouraged."

RESPONDING ACCURATELY TO SAD FEELINGS

In rare moments, our helpees might be "up," particularly when they have found some direction—however ten-
tative. Their whole demeanor changes. Their attitude
toward life opens up. Their behavior is intense and
rapid.

It is just as important to be able to respond to the
helpees in these moments as it is to respond to them in
their depressed moments. Indeed, it is ultimately more
important.

While it is critical to pick our helpees up at the level
that they are expressing themselves, we must ultimately
help them to move to new and more rewarding
behavior. We cannot help them to move if we cannot
respond to those rare moments of joy.

For many of us, these are the most difficult experiences to respond to. Sharing another's joy is difficult
indeed for those of us whose own moments of joy are
few and far between.

Sometimes our helpee's feelings are so intense that
he blurts them out: "I can't wait to get started!"

We might formulate a simple response to his feeling
state.

"You feel really excited."

RESPONDING ACCURATELY TO HAPPY FEELINGS

At times, the helpees might express other kinds of feelings which might be difficult to respond to. Sometimes they are just mad at the world, angry with its injustice and motivated to retaliate. Their bodies are tense, their eyes tearing and their expressions choked. Often we are afraid to open up such feelings. We are afraid of how far these feelings may carry them. "Will they act upon them?" "Will they act them out?" These are the questions which characterize our concern.

Nevertheless, we cannot help if we cannot deal with all of a person's feelings. Our helpee must get these feelings out in the open if he is going to learn to deal with them. Indeed, the probability of his acting upon angry feelings is inversely related to his ability to explore them. The more he explores them, the less likely he is to act destructively. Put another way, the more he explores them, the more likely he is to channel them constructively. Sometimes he expresses his feelings in violent terms: "I know damn well I'm going to get back at him any way I can!"

We may formulate a simple response to him.

"You feel furious."

RESPONDING ACCURATELY TO ANGRY FEELINGS

We must respond to our helpees in all their fullness—in their moments of sadness, happiness and anger. They are how they feel.

If we do not respond to our helpees in their fullness, the implications are clear: if we cannot find them, we lose them. If we lose them, they cannot find themselves.

There are many variations of feeling themes. Some major themes are surprise, fright, relief, distress, affection, disgust, interest and shame. There is a wide range of more specific feeling states to which we can respond.

We must learn to respond to these unique feelings. It is beneficial for both the helpers and the helpees to struggle to capture in words the uniqueness of the helpees' experiences.

Finding the most accurate feeling words may not be easy at first. You may say, "I just don't ordinarily use that many feeling words. I don't know if I can respond accurately." You will need to expand your feeling word vocabulary.

RESPONDING TO UNIQUE FEELINGS

The more feeling words we have available, the better our chances of accurately communicating our understanding of the helpees' unique experiences.

One effective way of organizing feeling words is to categorize them according to whether they are of high, medium or low intensity. Since the intensity of any word depends upon the person with whom it is used, we will need to visualize the typical helpees we work with to categorize by intensity level. Then we can discriminate both the feeling category and the level of intensity which we wish to employ. We may develop our own word list by filling in the next page. Appendix A contains an alphabetical listing of feeling words from which to draw. We may carry a list around with us and add to it. It will help us respond accurately.

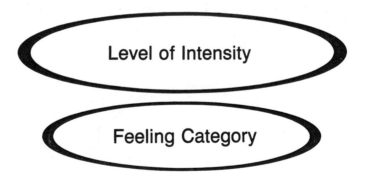

ACCURATE RESPONSE TO FEELING

Categories of Feelings*

Levels of Intensity	Happy	Sad	Angry	Scared	Confused	Strong	Weak
High	Excited Elated Overjoyed	Hopeless Depressed Devastated	Furious Seething Enraged	Fearful Afraid Threatened	Bewildered Trapped Troubled	Potent Super Powerful	Overwhelmed Impotent Vulnerable
Medium	Cheerful Up Good	Upset Distressed Sorry	Agitated Frustrated Irritated	Edgy Insecure Uneasy	Disorganized Mixed-Up Awkward	Energetic Confident Capable	Incapable Helpless Insecure
Low	Glad Content Satisfied	Down Low Bad	Uptight Dismayed Annoyed	Timid Unsure Nervous	Bothered Uncomfortable Undecided	Sure Secure Solid	Shaky Unsure Bored

*Since the intensity of any feeling word depends upon the person with whom it is used, you will need to visualize the typical helpee you work with to categorize these words by intensity level. (An Expanded Feeling Word List Is Found in Appendix A.)

Based upon the cues we receive from our observations and from the helpee's initial statements, we will attempt to determine the "general feeling category" of the helpee. Our next task is to finely tune our understanding of the helpee's feelings. We want to come up with feeling words that are interchangeable with our helpees experience. If we are having difficulty finding the "right words" but we know we are in the "ballpark," try this technique.

We begin by simply completing this statement, "When I feel _____ (general feeling), I feel _____ (specific feeling)." This will help us to come up with a more accurate interchangeable response to feeling.

For example, if the helpee says "I feel depressed" and we find ourselves at a loss for a new, more accurate word with which to respond, we might say to ourselves, "When I feel depressed I feel _____." We might complete this statement with "lost." "When I feel depressed, I feel lost." Look at and listen to the helpee. Does the helpee look and sound "lost?"

We continue to recycle this statement and check out the new feeling words until we have an interchangeable feeling word.

Again, we may wish to practice responding to feelings. We can respond to real life situations or recordings. The case studies and the student workbook may provide helpful stimulus materials for formulating feeling responses.

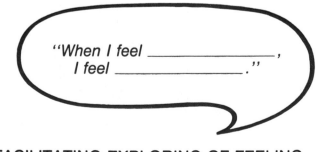

"When I feel _____,
I feel _____."

FACILITATING EXPLORING OF FEELING

Responding to Meaning

Responding to the feeling or the content of the helpees' expressions is not enough. Our response must be enriched by putting the feeling together with the content for the helpees.

Content is used to make the feeling meaningful. The content gives intellectual meaning to the helpees' expressions of their experiences. The feeling gives emotional meaning to the helpees' expressions of their experiences. Responding to meaning emphasizes making interchangeable responses that capture both the feeling and content of the expressions.

RESPONDING TO MEANING

Respond Interchangeably

Capture Content and Feeling

Remember, feelings are about content. The content provides the reason for the feeling. For example, let us look at several feeling states and related content areas.

Feeling	Content
Happy	about being promoted
Angry	with my teacher for giving me a low grade
Sad	when I knew that I'd never see her again

We may practice responding to meaning by determining the feeling and content of different experiences in our own lives.

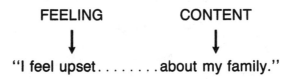

FEELING   CONTENT

"I feel upset . . . . about my family."

FEELINGS ABOUT CONTENT

A response to meaning is not complete until it communicates both feeling and content. Understanding of the helpees' expressions can be communicated by complementing a response to feeling with a response to content. For example, whereas "You're saying that _____" expressed the content of the helpee's expression and "You feel _____" expressed the helpee's feelings, "You feel _____ because _____" captures both the feeling and the content. This is an effective format for a complete interchangeable response to the helpee.

"You feel _____ because _____."

RESPONDING INTERCHANGEABLY

It is as if we try to understand with our minds what the helpees feel in their guts. We do this first by crawling inside of their feelings. Secondly, we comprehend the reason for the feelings expressed in their content.

Whereas "You feel sad" expressed the helpee's feelings with the passing of a loved one, "You feel sad because she was the most important person in the world to you and now she is gone" captures the meaning in the feeling and the content.

"You feel sad because she is gone."

CAPTURING BOTH THE FEELING AND THE CONTENT

If we do not respond to the content of the helpees' expressions, we will often find ourselves unable to work with their problems. Things that we can frame in our minds are easier to do something about than those which we only feel.

Let us spend a moment with our helpee. He states, "I'm just so angry at them. First they give me the opportunity and then they take it away. I missed my chance." Let's formulate a response that reflects both the feeling and content expressed by Tom.

Sometimes the helpees express multiple feelings and content. It is important for us to attend to all of the major feelings and contents.

"You feel furious because they cheated you out of a real chance and you feel sad because the opportunity is lost."

RESPONDING TO MANY FEELINGS AND CONTENTS

If we respond accurately to our helpees' expressions, we will involve them in exploring themselves in the areas in which they are having difficulty. Because we have understood Tom accurately at the level that he has presented himself, he will go on to share many other personal experiences of this and other situations.

He will also bring his friends around because we are good helpers. It is time to meet some of these friends— one is Joan, a cautious young woman. As a young woman growing into adulthood, she is increasingly aware of the differences in her experiences from those of young men. She is also increasingly aware of personal conflicts in choosing a professional career.

While we attend to Joan, she is reserved. She looks us over carefully. We might formulate an effective response, even though she has not said much.

> "You feel unsure of me because I might not be able to understand you."

RESPONDING TO DIFFICULT FEELINGS AND CONTENTS

Another of our helpee's is Floyd—an expressive young man. Floyd is black. Just as being a woman makes a difference in experience, so does being black, as does anything that makes us stand out. Floyd is assertive in expressing this: "I don't need this stuff. You can never know what it's like to be me!" We might formulate an effective response to Floyd's expression.

"You feel doubtful because I can't ever really know your experience."

The important thing is to enter the helpees' frames of reference to understand the feeling and content which they have expressed. Then we need to communicate that understanding at the level that they have expressed their concerns.

Joan may acknowledge the possibility that we might help her, but she is going to be cautious before involving herself. Floyd may acknowledge that we can help him but only if we acknowledge that there may be limits to the depth of our understanding.

There are as many responses as there are people. As helpers, we must learn to attend to all of these people and to break free of our own restrictive experiences to enter their worlds and individualize our responses.

We should continue to practice responding to other people whom we meet in our daily living. As we practice, our own skill level will increase and we will be better prepared to enter the frames of reference of others.

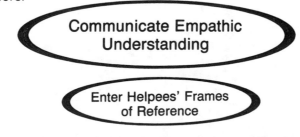

Communicate Empathic Understanding

Enter Helpees' Frames of Reference

FACILITATING EXPLORING OF MEANING

Summary

We can measure the accuracy of our responses based on feedback from the helpees. If the helpees continue to explore then we have been accurate in understanding and communicating what they have said. If we are not accurate in our responses we cannot help them explore their experiences.

We can measure the comprehensiveness of our responding with the following scale:

High responsiveness — Accurate inter-changeable response to feeling and content, meaning

Moderate responsiveness — Accurate inter-changeable response to feeling

Low responsiveness — Accurate inter-changeable response to content

Low levels of responsiveness are consistent with the high levels of attentiveness (listening and repeating ver-batim). The moderate levels of responsiveness involve responding to feeling. High levels of responsiveness involve responding to feeling and content, meaning.

Now we can continue to build our own cumulative rating scale for helping. If the helper is attentive and responsive to meaning (feeling and content) we can rate the helper at a fully-responsive level (level 3.0). If the helper responds to feeling alone, we can rate the helper at a partially-responsive level (level 2.5). If the helper is attending personally, observing and listening but responding to only the content of the helpees' expressions, we can rate the helper at less than a facilitative level (level 2.0).

At this point you may want to go back to case study #3 "Unskilled Responding" and rate the helper responses. Then write some of your own accurate and interchangeable responses, responses that would have been more facilitative.

LEVELS OF HELPING

5.0	
4.5	
4.0	
3.5	
3.0	Responding to meaning
2.5	Responding to feeling
2.0	Responding to content
1.5	Attending personally
1.0	Nonattending

LEVELS OF HELPING—
ATTENDING AND RESPONDING

The function of responding to the helpees' experiences is to facilitate their self-exploration of areas of concern. As helpers, we understand that there is no value to exploration unless it facilitates an understanding that goes beyond the material presented. Helpees, however, must explore where they are in order to understand where they want to be.

When the helpees become able to explore themselves, their feelings, content, and meaning the helpees signal a readiness for the next goal of learning and helping, understanding. This readiness for understanding signals helpers to begin personalizing.

PHASES OF HELPING

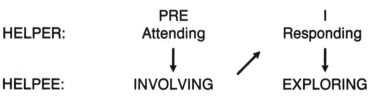

	PRE	I
HELPER:	Attending	Responding
HELPEE:	INVOLVING	EXPLORING

FACILITATING INVOLVING AND EXPLORING

You now know something about attending and responding skills. You can practice by forming your own responses to the helpee in the following case study. You can also practice by responding to the other case studies in this book and by trying the exercises in the student workbook. Additionally you can practice with classmates and friends. You will want to continue practicing these skills until you have integrated them into your helping personality.

Case Study #4—Skilled Responding

Carol Lewis is a 34-year-old woman. She is the mother of three children, a set of identical twin 4-year-old boys, Adam and Aaron, and a 6-year-old daughter, Nancy. Carol was widowed when her husband, Mark, died of a malignant brain tumor.

During his last few weeks, Mark was in a hospital. The last four days he was in a coma. Carol stayed at the hospital with him the last five days of his life, leaving the children with her parents.

The Lewis' were assigned to David Biloxi, a hospital social worker. Following is an excerpt of a conversation between David and Carol the day before Mark died. The conversation took place in a private lounge on Mark's ward.

David: "Let's sit down here." (Gestures to the couch). "Would you like some juice or something to eat?"

Carol: (sitting down) "No, I'm not hungry."

David: "You're looking pretty tired."

Carol: "I just haven't been able to sleep much."

David: "This is really a difficult time for you."

Carol: "I'm still not able to believe it's happening. I mean, a month ago we were planning to buy a new house. Mark had just gotten a promotion. And now, any minute he'll be . . . he'll be . . . gone. Dead."

David: "The whole thing is still unreal. A few weeks ago, the two of you were planning for the future together. Now, Mark is dying."

Carol: "It's so unbelievably unfair!" (shaking her head and clenching her fist).

David: "You're really angry about it all."

Carol: "I'm so damn mad! Damn mad! God . . . I just don't understand."

David: "You're furious because of the unjustness of Mark's dying."

Carol: "And the worst part is I'm so angry with God and the doctors and everybody."

David: "You're so enraged by what's happening that everyone becomes a target."

Carol: "Yes. And the horrible thing is . . . (she starts to cry) . . . "I'm so angry with Mark for leaving me. Sometimes I don't know if I can forgive him."

David: "You're especially angry with Mark because he's leaving you, abandoning you."

Carol: (crying harder) "That's right. I just don't know what I'll do without him . . . I love him so much . . . Mark . . . Mark . . . Oh God!"

David: (taking Carol into his arms and holding her as she sobs) "It really hurts having him die because of how much he means to you."

Carol: "He's been my life . . . even more than the children. With him gone, everything will be so empty. I'll be so . . . alone."

David: "You're frightened because you're going to be alone, having to live without Mark."

Carol: "That's it! That's why I'm so angry. I'm scared of being left alone. How could he do this to me!"

David: "You're frightened because you will have to start over."

6.
PERSONALIZING—
FACILITATING UNDERSTANDING

This chapter addresses the skill of personalizing. We will learn how to personalize meaning, feelings, problems and goals to facilitate helpees' understanding of their experiences.

Here are some questions that you can ask as you begin to think about personalizing:

How do you know when people have shown that they truly understand the significance of an important experience in your life?

How do you know when someone has correctly inferred something from what you have said?

How do you know when someone has helped you identify problems and goals in your life?

Read this case study and try to identify instances when the helper does not facilitate helpee understanding.

Case Study #5—Unskilled Personalizing

Bill Huachuca is a 21-year-old student. He is a journalism major with one more year of schooling to complete. For the last 18 months he has been seeing the same woman, Lisa, a 19-year-old medical technician major.

Bill came to the school's counseling center because Lisa had told Bill that she didn't want to see him anymore. She wanted to be free to "party", Bill subsequently tried to talk with Lisa who told him that she found him to be "lazy, boring, dull" and not to call her again. Bill became depressed and sought help after he had gone out with a friend, gotten drunk, and spent the rest of the night crying and shouting things like, "Lisa don't leave me, I love you!"

Bill has been seeing Tom Travis, a counseling intern working at the center. The following excerpt is from their second session together.

Bill: "I just can't get Lisa off my mind. I can't study. I can't work. I don't eat or sleep. All I do is think of Lisa! Lisa!"

Tom: "You're saying that your relationship with Lisa is the only thing you can focus on right now."

Bill: "Right, I can't stand being without her. I don't know if I can make it without her."

Tom: "You're really feeling scared because she's left you."

Bill: "I wish I knew what I did wrong!"

Tom: "You're angry because she won't continue to see you."

Bill: "She thinks I'm a bore, that I'm dull. She doesn't believe I have anything to offer."

Tom: "You're feeling guilty because she doesn't find you exciting."

Bill: "I guess I am a little dull. I mean I really live a quiet kind of life."

Tom: "You're saying you see your life as quiet and can understand how that might be dull for Lisa."

Bill: "Yeah, she wants to go out partying and drinking. She likes crowds and dancing and all that kind of stuff. I just don't enjoy it. I'd rather be home relaxing. I need my privacy."

Tom: "You're saying that you and Lisa want to do different kinds of things."

Bill: "I just don't know how to be the kind of person she wants to be with. I wish I did."

Tom: "You feel hurt because Lisa wants a different kind of person from the one you are."

Bill: "It's more than that, I guess; but I'm not sure what."

Tom: "You're saying there is more to your discouragement than not being able to meet Lisa's expectations."

Bill: "Yeah, I got a feeling that I wasn't, well . . . as exciting a lover as she wanted."

Tom: "You're saying you're unsure about yourself as a lover."

Bill: "Right, I don't know if I've got what it takes to, you know, turn women on."

Tom: "You're feeling scared because you don't know if you're exciting enough."

Bill: "Yeah, right! And I can't do anything about it. I'm a dull person and a lousy lover. Maybe I should become a priest or something."

Tom: "You feel discouraged and embarrassed because you can't change the way you are."

Bill: "Maybe Lisa is right about leaving me."

Tom: "You're saying you understand why Lisa left you."

Bill: "I just don't think I'll ever be any different."

Tom: "You feel disgusted because you don't think you can be any different."

Bill: "Do you know of any superstud pills I could take?"

Tom: "Well, no I don't Bill. But I think we're really making progress here. You're saying some really personal things and they're very important. I'm sure if we keep on talking we'll get somewhere."

Bill: "Well, okay, but we've been through this all before."

Tom: "You're saying we're covering the same ground again and that's right. But we're talking about these things a little differently. I think we're getting to some kind of understanding."

Bill: "Maybe you're right."

Personalizing is the most critical dimension for human change or gain. It is so critical because it emphasizes internalizing the helpees' responsibilities for their own problems. It involves building on the interchangeable base to go beyond the material expressed by the helpees. When we add accurately to the expressions of the helpees, we are facilitating their understanding of where they are in relation to where they want or need to be.

By personalizing the meaning we communicate the personal implications for the helpees. Personalizing problems emphasizes the helpees' ability to internalize responsibility for their deficits. This leads directly to personalized goals implied by the deficits. Personalizing also involves recycling the new feelings attendant to the personalized meaning, problems and goals. Personalizing facilitates helpee understanding and prepares us for initiating helpee action.

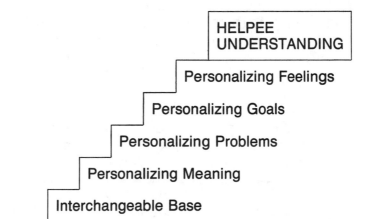

PERSONALIZING FACILITATES
HELPEE UNDERSTANDING

Interchangeable Base

Before we can move on to personalizing, we must establish a base of communication. Responding interchangeably to the helpees' expressions insures that we understand each of the helpees' expressions at the level presented. When we have made responses that incorporate accurately the feeling and meaning expressed by the helpees, we say that we have established an interchangeable base of communication.

In building an interchangeable base of communication, we may find it expedient to ask questions to fill certain "gaps" in our understanding. When we ask a question, we should follow it with a response. Indeed, the test of a good question is whether we can respond accurately to the helpees' answers. The skilled helper will sandwich questions between two interchangeable responses. Of course, if we find ourselves asking two consecutive questions without responding, then in all probability we have asked bad questions and should return to responding accurately.

In building an interchangeable base of communication, the helpees will inform us directly through their behaviors of their readiness to move on to additive levels. They alert us by demonstrating their ability to sustain self-exploratory behavior and to respond accurately to their own expressions. In other words, the helpees inform us of their readiness for movement to the next level by doing for themselves the things that we have been doing for them.

"You feel _____ because _____."

**BUILDING AN INTERCHANGEABLE
BASE OF COMMUNICATION**

Personalizing Meaning

Personalizing meaning is the first step toward facilitating the helpees' understanding of where they are in relation to where they want or need to be. We personalize the meaning when we relate the meaning directly to the helpees' experiences. In other words, we zero in on why the experiences are significant for the helpees.

In responding to meaning, we answered the question, "What is the situation and how do the helpees feel about it?" Now we answer the question, "What is the effect of the situation upon the helpees?"

Personalizing the meaning involves identifying common themes, internalizing experiences and personalizing implications. The common themes provide the basis for making personalized responses. Internalizing experience emphasizes making the helpees accountable for their experiences. Personalizing implications emphasizes developing the personal implications for the helpees.

PERSONALIZE MEANING

Personalize Implications

Internalize Experiences

Identify Common Themes

PERSONALIZING MEANING

Personalized responses are always formulated from the helpees' frames of reference. They acknowledge the helpees' experiences of the world and build upon those experiences. Just as we formulated meaning responses to individual helpee expressions, we now formulate personalized meaning responses to the helpees' expressions made over a period of time.

We do this by looking for the common themes in the helpees' expressions. The themes relate to what the helpees are saying about themselves. The common themes are derived from the extended base of communication. They are those themes which are interwoven through more than one of the helpees' expressions. When one common theme stands out above others because of recurrence or intensity, we may call it a dominant theme. In responding to the common or dominant theme, we may use the format:

"You feel _____ because things are always _____."

"You feel furious because things are always interfering."

IDENTIFYING COMMON THEMES

The common themes may then be personalized by internalizing the helpees' experiences. So often we find that helpees are talking about third persons—other friends, students, teachers, spouses, parents, children— about whom we can do nothing directly. By focusing upon others, the helpees are externalizing their experiences. By focusing upon themselves, the helpees internalize their experiences.

When responding to meaning, we used the format, "You feel _____ because _____ ." Now we internalize the meaning of their experiences by introducing the helpees to the response: "You feel _____ because **you** _____ ."

For example, when our helpee expressed his experience of his lost opportunity, we may have responded to meaning like this: "You feel furious because the opportunity is gone." Now we may personalize the meaning by internalizing the experience for the helpee.

"You feel furious because you got cheated."

INTERNALIZING EXPERIENCES

The key ingredient in personalizing meaning is considering the personal implications for the helpees. We do this by asking, "Why are these experiences important for the helpees?" Put another way, "How have the helpees' experiences impacted them?" We are looking at the consequences of their experiences for the helpees.

In personalizing the meaning, we may use the format, "You feel _____ because you _____ (personal implications)." We may personalize the implications for any living, learning and working experience.

After asking the personal implications question, we may make a personalized response to our helpee's experience of a lost opportunity.

"You feel furious because you are always getting left behind."

PERSONALIZING IMPLICATIONS

We must continue to check back with the helpees to stay in tune with their experiences. In so doing, we may find that their feelings are changing. For example, realizing he has been left behind, the helpee may find himself feeling more frustrated or upset with himself then furious with other people. If we do not have a precisely-accurate feeling response, we continue to cycle the feeling question: "How does that make me feel?" We may continue to practice personalizing meaning in live or recorded interactions such as the case studies.

"You feel frustrated because you are always getting left behind."

PERSONALIZING FEELINGS ABOUT MEANING

Personalizing Problems

Personalizing problems is the most critical transitional step to action. It is from our problems that we derive our goals. It is from our goals that we derive our action programs.

Personalizing problems is based upon personalizing meaning. We personalize problems when we help the helpees to understand what they cannot do that has led to their present experience of themselves. In other words, we answer the question of personalized problems: "What is there about the helpees that is contributing to the problems?" In responding to personalized meaning, we looked at the personal impact of the situation upon the helpees. Now we are asking the helpees to take responsibility for their lives and to look at themselves as the source of their problems. Personalizing problems involves conceptualizing, internalizing and concretizing deficits.

PERSONALIZE PROBLEMS

Concretize Deficits

Internalize Deficits

Conceptualize Deficits

PERSONALIZING PROBLEMS

In conceptualizing the deficits, we ask the question: "What was missing that contributed to the problem?" The question is initially asked independent of the helpee. It is simply an attempt to ascertain the missing ingredient that might have contributed to the problem. Sometimes we are initially unaware of what that ingredient might be. We might have to search out expert information and people for advice.

In the illustration of our helpee's lost opportunity, some initiative was missing. Perhaps no one took the initiative to make the opportunity clear to him. Certainly, he did not take the initiative to take advantage of the opportunity. We may conceptualize the deficit by using the format: "You feel _____ because _____ was missing."

"You feel frustrated because initiative was missing."

CONCEPTUALIZING DEFICITS

To personalize we must internalize. Now we must internalize the deficits. This means making the helpees accountable or responsible for their roles in the deficits. They must ask and answer the internalizing question: "What is there about me that contributed to the problem?"

In responding to the internalized deficit for our helpee's lost opportunity, we may internalize the deficit by using the format: "You feel _____ because you cannot _____."

> "You feel frustrated because you cannot assume initiative."

INTERNALIZING DEFICITS

Finally, it is important to concretize the deficit. If we can concretize the deficit, then we will be able to concretize the goal and, thus, make it achievable. In concretizing the deficit, we answer the question: "How can we observe or measure the deficit?"

In personalizing the problem, we formulate a response that defines the helpee's deficit behaviors. The statement of the helpee deficit must be in concrete behavioral terms if it is to be effective. Use the format, "You feel _____ because you cannot _____."

In concretizing our helpee's initiative deficit, we may observe or measure the deficit by an inability to take programmatic steps to take advantage of an opportunity when it arises. In concretizing deficits, we may use the format: "You feel _____ because you cannot _____."

"You feel frustruated because you cannot take the right steps at the right time."

CONCRETIZING DEFICITS

Again, we will want to personalize the new feelings attendant to the personalized problem. Personalizing the feelings emphasizes responding to how the helpees feel about themselves in relation to their deficits. When helpees internalize a deficit their feelings about themselves and their experiences will often change. We continue to ask the empathy question, "How does that make me feel?" For example, feelings of pain or hurt or weakness or vulnerability may become feelings of self-disappointment because the helpees lack the responses to handle their situations. Similarly, our helpee feels disappointed because of his lack of initiative.

"You feel disappointed in yourself because you lack initiative."

PERSONALIZING FEELINGS ABOUT DEFICITS

Sometimes we may choose to expedite personalizing problems through confrontations. Confrontations may take many forms. We may confront the helpees with behaviors that disagree with what they say. Sometimes we point to a discrepancy between how the helpees say they feel and how they look. A discrepancy might exist between how the helpees really are and how they want to be or how they want to be seen. Or a discrepancy may exist between insight and action.

In making our confrontations, it is usually most effective to use the format for a mild confrontation: "On the one hand, you say/feel/do _____ while on the other hand you say/feel/do _____." When such confrontations are made **in the context of a personalized relationship**, they may serve to promote open-ended inquiries into the behaviors. An effective confrontation is always followed by an effective helper response. Remember, confrontations are never necessary and never sufficient. However, in the hands of an effective helper, they may be efficient tools to recycle further exploration and understanding.

"You say you feel frustrated by your lack of initiative, but you don't do anything about it."

CONFRONTING DEFICITS

Personalizing Goals

Personalizing goals is the simplest transitional step. If we have personalized the problem effectively, then we should be able to personalize the goal fluidly.

Personalizing goals involves establishing where the helpees want to be in relation to where they are. The basic way to personalize goals is to determine the behaviors that are the opposite of the personalized problem. Thus, the goal can be described as the "flip side" of the problem. Personalizing goals involves conceptualizing, internalizing, and concretizing desired or needed assets.

```
                        ┌─────────────────────┐
                        │  PERSONALIZE GOALS  │
                   ┌────┘─────────────────────┘
                   │ Concretize Assets
              ┌────┘
              │ Internalize Assets
         ┌────┘
         │ Conceptualize Assets
```

PERSONALIZING GOALS

Just as we conceptualized the deficits, so do we now conceptualize the desired assets. We simply reverse the question by asking: "What might contribute to resolving the problem?" Usually, we can find the desired assets by directly reversing the deficits. Thus, an interpersonal deficit implies an interpersonal asset. Similarly, an initiative deficit implies an initiative asset. In other words, the goal behavior can be defined as the opposite or "flip side" of the problem behavior. In conceptualizing assets, you may use the format: "You feel _____ because you cannot _____ and you want to _____."

"You feel disappointed because you cannot initiate, and you want to initiate."

CONCEPTUALIZING ASSETS

Sometimes it is still very difficult for the helpees to internalize desired assets. They may understand the logic but are unable to experience themselves with the assets. At this point, it may be necessary to recycle exploring and understanding in order to come to grips with the helpees' potential for learning to develop these assets. We will want to establish an extensive base of interchangeable responses exploring their inability to internalize potential assets. As the helpees explore their experiences we will modify the personalized goals, staying in tune with the helpees. When we finally internalize the desired assets, we may use the format: "You feel _____ because you cannot _____ and you really want to _____."

"You feel disappointed because you cannot initiate, and you really want to learn to initiate."

INTERNALIZING ASSETS

We will want to concretize potential desired assets just as we concretized deficits. Again, we may need to search out some sources of expertise in concretizing these assets. When we concretize the assets, we are making the goals achievable. We are beginning to determine which specific assets will be needed to achieve the helpees' goals.

For example, with our helpee, we may measure initiative assets as an ability to take programmatic steps at opportune times. In concretizing assets, we may use the formula: "You feel _____ because you cannot _____ and you really want to _____."

"You feel disappointed because you cannot initiate, and you really want to be able to develop and implement initiative programs."

CONCRETIZING ASSETS

Just as we personalized feelings about deficits or problems, so do we personalize feelings about assets or goals. Similarly, just as "down" feelings are usually attached to problems, so are "up" feelings or feelings of happiness usually attached to goals. Thus, the helpees usually become hopeful for their futures or pleased with having a direction in life. We continue to ask the empathy question, "How does that make me feel?" In personalizing feelings about goals, we may use the format: "You feel _____ because you are going to _____."

"You feel eager because you are going to learn to initiate."

PERSONALIZING FEELINGS ABOUT ASSETS

Sometimes the helpees are reluctant to deal with their assets. Depending upon their life experiences, many helpees are more afraid of succeeding than they are of failing. They may be familiar with failing. At some level they may have accommodated failure in their lives with some comfort. If appropriate and expeditious, we may confront strengths as well as weaknesses, assets as well as deficits. In making our confrontations, we may use the format for mild confrontations. We must be sure to respond accurately and extensively to the effects of these confrontations in order to recycle exploring and understanding. Remember, the confrontations are only effective and economical in the hands of a skilled helper.

"You say you are unsure about achieving your goals yet you recognize your strengths for achieving them."

CONFRONTING ASSETS

Summary

One way of structuring personalizing is to test the comprehensiveness and accuracy of our personalized response to the helpees' expressions. We can begin by simply attending and responding interchangeably in our next encounter. Then offer some personalized responses. We can rate the accuracy of our personalizing the helpees' experiences as follows:

High personalizing	— Accurately personalized problems, feelings and goals incorporating helpee's response deficits and assets
Moderate personalizing	— Accurately personalized meaning incorporating personal implications of experience
Low personalizing	— Accurate responsiveness to meaning

As can be seen, the low levels of personalizing are consistent with the high levels of responsiveness (feeling and content). The moderate levels of personalizing involve meaning, while the high levels involve the problems, feelings and goals.

LEVELS OF PERSONALIZING

We can continue to build our cumulative scale for helping. If the helper is attending, responding and personalizing the problem, feelings and goal for the helpee, we
can rate the helper at a fully-personalizing level (level
4.0). If the helper is attentive and responsive and personalizes the meaning for the helpee, we can rate the
helper at a facilitatively-personalizing level (level 3.5).

LEVELS OF HELPING

5.0
4.5
4.0   Personalizing problem, feeling and goal
3.5   Personalizing meaning
3.0   Responding to meaning
2.5   Responding to feeling
2.0   Responding to content
1.5   Attending
1.0   Nonattending

LEVELS OF HELPING—
ATTENDING, RESPONDING AND PERSONALIZING

Formulating an effective personalized response is the key to helping. If we can enter the helpees' frames of reference and enable them to see things clearly, we will help them take the major steps in changing their behaviors. If we cannot do so, the helpees will not have the perspective necessary for developing directions that lead out of their difficulty.

As we move to personalized levels of responding, we are, as we have seen, automatically introducing our own experience. That is, we are going beyond what the helpees have expressed. We must be drawing from our own experience, our knowledge of assets and deficits, our understanding of the content, and our understanding of the helpee.

We can practice personalizing by practicing some of the exercises in the student workbook or by forming responses to the case studies in this book. The best practice, however, will come from working with our classmates and associates. Practice personalizing less intense helpee experiences before attempting to use the skills in intense helping situations.

The key to formulating effective personalized responses is discipline. This includes discipline in building an interchangeable base, in using that base to search out the common or dominant themes, and in personalizing feeling, meaning, problems, and goals. The effectiveness of our formulations may be determined by how well the helpees utilize our personalized attempts.

PHASES OF HELPING

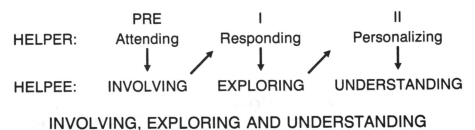

INVOLVING, EXPLORING AND UNDERSTANDING

You now know about attending, responding and personalizing skills. You will need to work most intensely on your personalizing skills because they are most difficult to learn. Practice until you can process these responses easily, as the helper does in the following case study.

Case Study #6—Skilled Personalizing

Barbara Dix is a 25-year-old graduate student who will complete her masters degree in physics next semester. However, in the last few months she has become unsure of her desire to be a physicist. She already has several job offers when she graduates but has deferred making a decision.

She has sought help from Debbie, an old roommate and friend who is now working in the University's placement office. The following excerpt takes place after two previous sessions and well into the third session.

Barb: "When I realized that the reason I went on with school was to prove to my family that I could do it, I also realized that being a physicist might not be what I really want to do."

Debbie: "You went on to get your masters to prove yourself to your family and now you're not sure if that's what you really want to do."

Barb: "I get so upset with the way they discount me because I'm a girl. They always put my brothers first."

Debbie: "You feel angry because they have never accepted you as an equal to your brothers."

Barb: "The entire thing is just so stupid! I keep trying to prove to them I'm worthy, and no matter what I do they'll never accept me."

Debbie: "You feel disgusted because they can't recognize what you can do."

Barb: "Yes. Why can't I be satisfied with me knowing what I can do?"

Debbie: "You're angry because you haven't been able to break free from wanting to earn their approval."

Barb: "That's right! I can't be satisfied with myself or what I do because I want their respect."

Debbie: "You feel disgusted with yourself because you have let your need for their respect determine what you do with your life."

Barb: "And now at twenty-five, three months away from a masters in physics, I'm not sure if I really want to be a physicist or if I'm doing it solely to earn their love."

Debbie: "You feel scared because you can't be sure that becoming a physicist is something you really want to do or something you're doing to earn your family's love."

Barb: "I need to find out if I've made a big mistake."

Debbie: "You're unsure about what your own career needs are."

Barb: "Yeah. I'm not even sure how to make such an important decision myself."

Debbie: "You feel discouraged because you can't assert your own needs as indicated by your inability to make a decision."

Barb: "That's a pretty pathetic description of someone about to get her masters, but I guess it's accurate. I just kept doing what I thought my folks wanted and now here I am. . . ."

Debbie: "You're embarrassed by your inability to assert yourself and live your own life."

Barb: "Right. And I think it's about time I do something about that."

Debbie: "You're disappointed in yourself because you don't know how to make decisions and you want to learn to do so."

Barb: "Exactly! When I know how to make my own decisions then I'll know if I'm living my own life or just trying to prove something to my parents."

Debbie: "Now you're energized by the thought of taking control of your life. You want to learn to assert your own needs as indicated by knowing and acting upon the skills of decision making."

7.
INITIATING—FACILITATING ACTING

This chapter addresses the skills of initiating. We will learn how to define goals, develop programs and initiate programs. This will facilitate the helpees' ability to act upon their experiences.

Here are some questions you can ask as you begin to think about initiating:

How do you know when you have reached your goal?

How do you know when you are moving toward your goal?

How do you know when someone is assisting you in achieving your goal?

Read this case study and try to identify instances when the helper does not facilitate helpee acting.

Case Study #7—Unskilled Initiating

Carol Snelling is an attractive 31-year-old woman. She has been married for twelve years and has two girls aged twelve and ten. Carrying a large suitcase, Carol has come to a crisis intervention center with her two children. She has several bruises on her arms and one on her face, accompanied by a recent gash over her left eye. One of her daughters has recently had a bloody nose and one of her eyes is bruised. Carol originally came to the center because she and her children left home due to her husband's physical and emotional abuse. She was placed in a Battered Women's Shelter and returned to the center the next day to talk more extensively with a counselor.

Her counselor, Meg Mitchell, has been doing family counseling for several years. The following is an excerpt from their first session. The children are not present.

Carol: "It got so bad that I had to take the kids and leave. At first Steve just shouted. Then he started hitting me. Then he hit the kids. And, it was happening more and more often. . . .

(crying) I don't know what it is I do that sets him off. I've tried, but I always seem to do something wrong.''

Meg: "You're feeling guilty because Steve told you that you were the reason he was upset."

Carol: "That's right! He would yell at me or the kids about something and then he'd work himself into a frenzy. I'd get so scared. I'm worried right now because of what he might do if he finds me."

Meg: "You're feeling scared because he still might hurt you or the children."

Carol: "Maybe I shouldn't have left. He's going to be so upset. . . .''

Meg: "You're feeling scared of what he might do and guilty because you left him."

Carol: "I know it sounds confusing, but I can't help it. I still love him! I just don't know how to keep him happy."

Meg: "You feel guilty because you love Steve but can't please him. You don't know what it is that you're doing wrong."

Carol: "Yes. But at the same time he shouldn't be beating me or the kids. That's wrong, too!"

Meg: "You're furious with Steve for his violence."

Carol: "I don't know who's more to blame. I know I'm not the best wife in the world. He's not the greatest husband. The kids can be a little much sometimes too."

Meg: "You feel overwhelmed because you don't know who exactly is responsible for what. All you know is that everyone has a part of the responsibility."

Carol: "That's right. Each of us has been doing something wrong."

Meg: "You feel miserable because you know that the family members have been hurting each other but you can't figure out how to change things."

Carol: "It's just beyond me. The whole thing becomes so confusing."

Meg: "You feel disappointed because you can't figure out how to get the family members to relate to one another the way they should."

Carol: "That's right."

Meg: "Carol, what you want, then, is to have you, Steve and the children build the kind of family relationships that will let everyone grow."

Carol: "Exactly what I want. But how do I do that?"

Meg: "You're saying that you don't know how to do that."

Carol: "Everything is such a mess that I don't know where to begin."

Meg: "Well, there isn't much we can do unless Steven and the kids get involved in therapy."

Carol: "Steve would never see a counselor. . . . He'd refuse. He thinks all shrinks are crazy. Oh, excuse me."

Meg: "That's all right, but without Steve we won't be able to accomplish anything. You're going to have to figure out a way to get him here."

Carol: "I don't think there's anything I can do to make him come. I don't know. . . ."

Meg: "You have to try."

Carol: "All right, but what if he refuses?"

Meg: "Let's wait and see if you can get him here. O.K.?"

Carol: "Well, O.K."

Initiating is the culminating phase of helping. Initiating emphasizes facilitating the helpees' efforts to act to achieve their goals. In other words, the helpees act to change or gain in their functioning. This action is based upon their personalized understanding of their goals. It is facilitated by the helper's initiative.

Initiating involves defining goals, developing programs, designing schedules and reinforcements and individualizing steps. Initiating also includes preparing to implement steps and initiate check steps.

Defining the goals emphasizes the operations comprising the goals. Developing programs emphasizes the steps needed to achieve the goals. Designing schedules emphasizes attaching time to steps while designing reinforcements emphasizes attaching reinforcements to steps. Individualizing emphasizes insuring that the steps are related to the helpees' frames of reference. Preparing to implement the steps involves reviewing, rehearsing and revising. Then the helpees are ready to check their progress by using "before, during and after check steps."

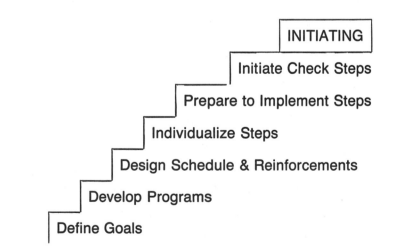

INITIATING

Initiate Check Steps

Prepare to Implement Steps

Individualize Steps

Design Schedule & Reinforcements

Develop Programs

Define Goals

INITIATING FACILITATES HELPEE ACTING

Defining Goals

The first task in initiating is defining the goal. If we can define the goal then our direction is clear.

In defining the goal we need to establish all of the ingredients necessary to achieve the goal. We accomplish this by defining the 5WH and by defining a standard to measure the basic question of direction. "How will we know when we have reached our goal?"

> **GOAL DEFINED**
>
> Define Standards
>
> Define 5WH of Behavior

We need to determine all of the ingredients of our goal. It is important to include all of the people or things involved. Sometimes third parties or indirect experiences or tasks may impinge upon the helpees' achievement of the goals. We need to determine, "Who or what is involved?"

In defining the goal we need to include all of the activities involved. "What will be done?" That way no critical activity may be omitted in our attempts to achieve our goals.

It is also important to describe the reason for and methods to accomplish the goals. "Why and how will the goals be accomplished?"

We also need to describe when and where the activity will occur. It is important to be specific to insure that the helpee knows when and where the new behavior will take place.

For example: Bill feels disappointed because he cannot relate effectively with his parents and he really wants to learn how to relate effectively.

A defined goal will include information about the 5WH.

Who — Bill and his parents
What — will relate effectively
How and Why — by responding accurately to increase communication
When and Where — at home during mealtimes

DEFINE 5WH OF BEHAVIOR

In order to determine when the helpee has reached the goal we will need to define observable and measurable standards. Defining standards usually means describing the goal in terms of the number of times or amount of time the helpee is engaged in some behavior. We can define the standard by answering the question: "How well will it be done?"

For example, we need to determine a standard to measure how well Bill will perform.

How Well — by establishing an interchangeable base of communication with at least 6 responses

DEFINE STANDARDS

We must now communicate our definition of the goal to the helpee. We do this by emphasizing the behavior and the standards of performance.

In initating we define the goal by employing the format:

"You want to _____ (5WH of behavior) as indicated by _____ (standards)."

> *"You want to relate effectively by building an interchangeable base with your parents as indicated by six interchangeable responses at home during mealtimes."*

COMMUNICATING THE OPERATIONAL GOAL

Developing Programs

In order to achieve the goals, we need to develop programs. Programs are simply step-by-step procedures for achieving the goals. Given the definition of the goals, the programs are derived from the goals. Every step in the program should lead to accomplishing the goal.

Most programs are sequenced by contingency, i.e., each step is dependent upon the performance of the previous step. That is, we determine what steps we must perform as preconditions for the next step and, finally, the operations of the goal. In this context, an action program consists of an operational goal, a basic first step and the intermediary steps to the goal. The goal is where the helpees want or need to be. The first step is the most basic step beginning with where the helpees are. The intermediary steps are the steps that lead directly to the achievement of the goal. They bridge the gap from where the helpees are to where they want to be.

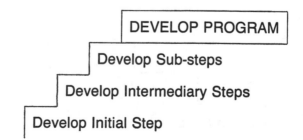

DEVELOP PROGRAM

Develop Sub-steps

Develop Intermediary Steps

Develop Initial Step

DEVELOPING PROGRAMS

The first step is the most basic step that the helpee must take. It should be the most fundamental building block in the program. That way we can build the other steps upon it. For example, if the goal is running a mile in eight minutes, the first step might be walking around the block. For some people the first step to running a mile may literally and physically be taking a first step.

For our helpee the first step in relating to his parents might be attending to them. In the learning or working area the first step may be attending to the task at hand. In communicating the first step, we use a simple straight-forward format.

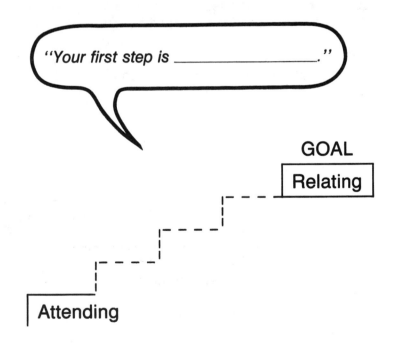

DEVELOPING INITIAL STEPS

Intermediary steps bridge the gap between the first step and the goal. Our first intermediary step should be approximately halfway between the first step and the goal. For example, if the goal is running a mile in eight minutes, the first intermediary step might be running one-half mile or running a mile in 12 minutes.

For our helpee the first intermediary step in relating to his parents might be listening to them. Similarly, the first intermediary step in learning might be understanding the learning goal while the first intermediary step in working might be developing the task requirements. In communicating the first intermediary step, we use a direct, simple format.

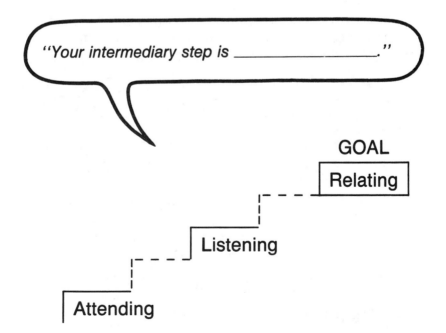

DEVELOPING INTERMEDIARY STEPS

We continue to fill out our program by developing sub-steps. We develop sub-steps by treating each step in the program as a sub-goal and developing the initial and intermediary steps to achieving that sub-goal. We continue to do this until we have all the steps needed to achieve our goal. If we leave out a step, our helpees will fail to achieve their goals. If we are planning to run a mile, we must develop distance and time substeps, moving, for example, from 1/4 to 1/2 to 3/4 to 1 mile and from 12 to 10 to 9 to 8 minutes.

With our helpee, the sub-steps to the goal of ''relating'' might emphasize observing and responding skills. In turn, these skills can be treated as sub-goals and sub-steps can be developed to achieve the sub-goals just as we have in this book. We might develop similar exploring and acting sub-steps for a learning program and sub-steps of expanding options and selecting preferred courses for a working program. In communicating the sub-steps, we use a simple format.

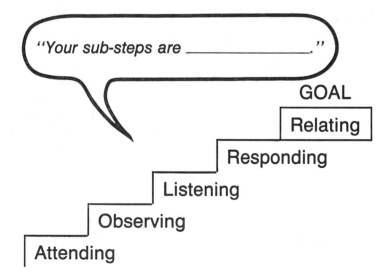

DEVELOPING SUB-STEPS

Developing Schedules

The process of initiating continues as we develop time schedules for step and goal achievement. Schedules serve to focus our programs. They close the gaps that might have been left by open-ended timeliness.

The major emphasis in scheduling is on developing starting times and finishing or completion times. They tell both helpers and helpees when things are to be done. Starting and finishing times may also be set for individual steps as well as for the overall program. No program is complete without starting times and completion times.

DEVELOP SCHEDULES

Determine Completion Times

Determine Starting Times

DEVELOPING SCHEDULES

The first step in developing schedules is setting specific starting times or dates. For example, we might start walking immediately to achieve our goal of running a mile in eight minutes.

With our helpee, we may set a starting time for the interpersonal skills program. We may set similar starting times for all living, learning and working steps and goals. In communicating starting times, we may use a simple and direct format.

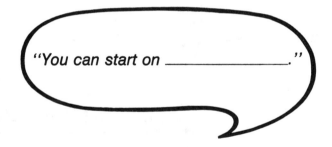

SETTING STARTING TIMES

The next step in developing schedules is setting specific completion times or dates. For example, we might set a completion time of six months for achieving our goal of running a mile in eight minutes.

In our illustration, our helpee may aim to complete the "relating" program by the end of month two. Again, we may set similar completion times for any living, learning and working steps or goals. In communicating completion times, we may use a simple format.

"You can finish on _____."

SETTING COMPLETION TIMES

In a similar manner, we can set starting and completion times for each interim step. The main purpose of setting schedules is to monitor the timeliness of the helpee's performance of the steps of the program. For example, our helpee might decide that he would spend the next month learning and practicing how to make accurate interchangeable responses. The first week he could concentrate upon attending, observing and listening; the second week upon responding to content; the third week upon responding to feeling; and the fourth week upon responding to feeling, content and meaning. A detailed schedule allows both helpee and helper to monitor the performance of steps.

"You can start _____ and finish in _____ ."

MONITORING TIMELINES

Developing Reinforcements

The next step in initiating involves developing reinforcements that will encourage the helpees to take the needed steps. Reinforcements are simply things that matter to us. They are most effective when they are applied immediately following our step performance.

The consequences of carrying out the steps to achieve goals and overcome deficits are often too distant for the helpees. More immediate reinforcements must be introduced.

Clearly, these reinforcements must come from the helpees' frames of reference. What we think matters for the helpees must really matter to them. Many helping programs have failed because of their inability to attach appropriate reinforcements. We all know stories of people who fuss to get attention because any attention— even negative—is more reinforcing than the reinforcements of their programs. In this context, we continue to emphasize our responsiveness: empathy is the source of all knowledge about powerful reinforcements for the helpees. Sometimes, it may be appropriate for helpees to work with support persons or groups to monitor their performance and administer the reinforcements.

> DEVELOP
> REINFORCEMENTS
>
> Determine Negative Reinforcements
>
> Determine Positive Reinforcements

DEVELOPING REINFORCEMENTS

Positive reinforcements or rewards are our most potent reinforcements. People tend to work hard for things that really matter to them. This means the helper must work diligently to develop the positive reinforcements from the helpees' frames of reference. In turn, the helpees must work diligently to receive the reinforcements.

Our helpee, for example, might decide simply that he would go out with his friends on Friday and Saturday nights as he successfully completed each step of his program. We can develop similar reinforcements for any and all living, learning and working programs. The reinforcements will vary as widely as the tastes of human nature itself.

"As you complete each step, you can _____."

REINFORCING POSITIVELY

To the degree we can, we want to avoid employing negative reinforcements. We use the term in a restricted sense to mean punishments. In this context, the application of negative reinforcements stimulates other reactions, such as aversive reactions to the person who administers the punishment. Initially, we should attempt to define the negative reinforcements as the absence of rewards.

In our helpee's case, he defined his own negative reinforcements as the absence of rewards. Specifically, he decided to stay home on the weekend to work on the uncompleted step in his program. Again, similar negative reinforcements may be designed and applied in other living, learning and working programs. Like rewards, negative reinforcements vary widely and, to use them effectively, we must be finely tuned to the people involved.

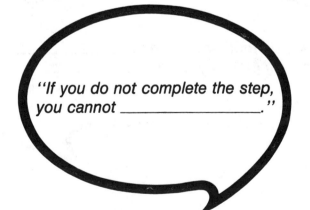

"If you do not complete the step, you cannot _____."

REINFORCING NEGATIVELY

If it is not clear whether a step was performed in a satis-factory manner, then we must vigilently observe the per-formers. We do so to determine whether the helpees are moving toward or away from the goals. Ultimately, all behavior is either goal-directed or not goal-directed.

Once we come to understand the helpees' behaviors we respond to positively reinforce the goal-directed behavior of our helpees and to negatively reinforce the negative, goal-less behavior. We are aligning ourselves with what is healthy in the individuals and opposing that which is unhealthy. We communicate our respect for them as people but not for their unhealthy behavior. We may use ourselves as potent reinforcers by being condi-tional. We can do this by spelling out the implications of the helpee's behavior for our own behavior.

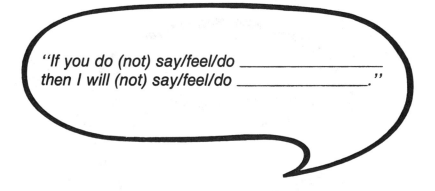

"If you do (not) say/feel/do _____
then I will (not) say/feel/do _____.*"

OBSERVING VIGILENTLY AND
REINFORCING CONDITIONALLY

Individualizing Steps

Most programs are comprised of steps that are sequenced by contingency, where each step is dependent upon the performance of the previous step. Some helpees cannot perform the steps readily as they are designed. They require programs individualized to their own particular learning or processing styles.

Every step of initiating should be individualized by checking back with the helpees. We check back with the helpees by making interchangeable responses that insure that we are in tune with the helpees' frames of reference. Even when we individualize the sequencing of steps, we must stay finely tuned because this is a very subtle human process.

Preparing to Implement Steps

Now that we are ready to implement the programs we find that there still are steps necessary before our final implementation. They are the final steps of preparation before implementation.

The critical implementation steps emphasize reviewing, rehearsing and revising the steps of the program. Reviewing insures the inclusiveness of our steps. Rehearsing helps us find the problems involved in implementing the steps. Revising emphasizes the final changes in the implementation program. Together, these steps prepare us for the implementation of the program. These detailed steps are necessary if we wish to succeed.

```
PREPARE TO
IMPLEMENT STEPS
```
Revise Steps

Rehearse Steps

Review Steps

PREPARING TO IMPLEMENT STEPS

The first implementation step emphasizes reviewing all the steps of the program. In so doing, we must review our definitions of goals, steps of programs, times of schedules, consequences of reinforcements and modalities of individualizing. For example, in our running program, we must check all distances and time steps.

In implementing the interpersonal relating program, our helpee must begin by reviewing all steps of attending personally, observing, listening and responding. Again, reviewing gives us a chance to make sure that we have included all necessary steps in the program.

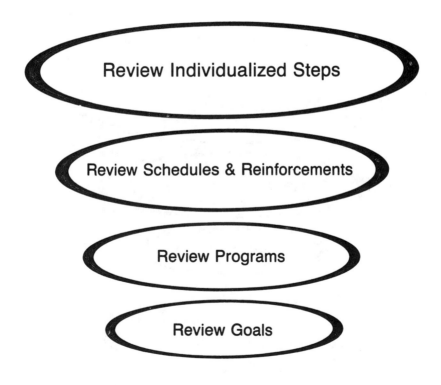

REVIEWING STEPS

The second implementation step emphasizes rehearsing all the steps of the program. In so doing, we get a chance to pilot our final performance. Rehearsing gives us the opportunity to find the problems involved in the final implementation of the steps. For example, in our running program, we can try ourselves out in real-life running situations.

In implementing the interpersonal relating program, our helpee may rehearse all of the attending and responding steps. Again, rehearsal is necessary if we care about being successful.

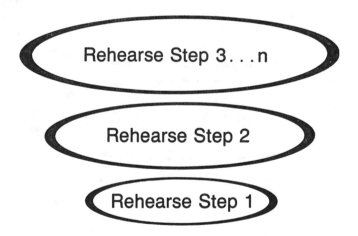

REHEARSING STEPS

The third implementation step emphasizes revising all necessary steps of the program. The purpose of reviewing and rehearsing is revising. In revising, we recycle all of the necessary revisions in the steps of the program. We will revise the program again, when we get the feedback from our action step. In our running program, we may revise our time and distance estimates upward and downward.

In implementing the interpersonal attending program, our helpee may revise some of the steps or sub-steps in order to increase the effectiveness of his action. Revising insures our probability of succeeding.

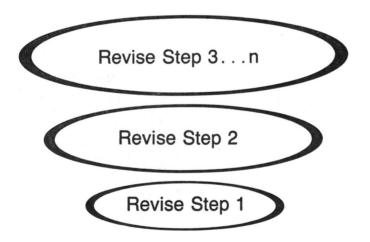

REVISING STEPS

Initiating Check Steps

Just when we think we are ready to act, we find that we need to develop more steps in our programs. If we plan "giant" steps we risk failure. To insure success we must develop detailed programs, with small achievable steps.

One of the ways of building in success is to develop check steps. Check steps emphasize the things we need to think about before, during and after the performance of each program step. They emphasize the resources we need to be successful and the ways to monitor and assess our effectiveness in performing the steps.

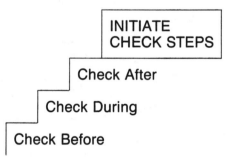

INITIATE
CHECK STEPS

Check After

Check During

Check Before

INITIATING CHECK STEPS

The "before check steps" emphasize the things we need to do before we perform each step. They ask and answer the question: "What resources will I need to perform the step successfully?" These resources include physical, emotional and intellectual resources. For example, in planning to run a mile, physically we need a measured distance and stopwatch as well as some appropriate kind of running shoes and clothes. Emotionally we need motivation for achieving our goal and intellectually we need a step-by-step program.

In implementing the interpersonal attending steps of the relating program, our helpee needs an appropriate physical setting and an occasion to interact with people such as that provided by mealtime in his home. In addition, he needs an emotional commitment and an intellectual program to achieve his goal. Without the resources, we are not able to perform the steps effectively. The "before check steps" give us an opportunity to check out our resources before performing the steps.

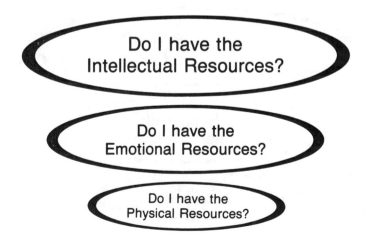

BEFORE CHECK STEPS

"During check steps" emphasize the things we need to do during the performance of each step. These check steps ask and answer the question: "Am I performing the step correctly?" Again, this involves physical, emotional and intellectual dimensions. Physically, in running, we may check our times and distances. Emotionally, we may check out our level of motivation. Intellectually, we may check whether we are running with proper form or appropriate breathing.

In implementing the interpersonal relating program, our helpee may check physically whether he is squared with others, sitting forward at a 20° angle and making eye contact. Emotionally, he may check whether he is being fully attentive to others. Intellectually, he may check whether he is focused on the content and feeling of the others' expressions. The "during check steps" give us an opportunity to check ourselves out during the performance of the steps.

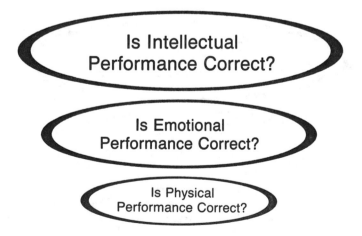

DURING CHECK STEPS

"After check steps" emphasize the things we need to do after the performance of each step. We ask and answer the question: "Did I achieve the results I wanted?" These are physical, emotional, and intellectual results and benefits. For example in implementing the running program we might check to see if we ran the intended distance within the targeted time and gained the physical benefits. Intellectually we may check any learnings gained from the achievement of the program step.

In implementing the interpersonal attending program, our helpee may check out whether he did or did not attend effectively. He may also check whether his attentiveness facilitated his parents' involvement in a conversation with him. He may check whether the conversation led to the desired benefits of improved relations.

AFTER CHECK STEPS

Summary

One way of structuring initiating is to test the comprehensiveness of our initiative responses to the helpees' experience. Let us simply attend, respond and personalize in our next encounter. Then let us attempt to rate the effectiveness of our initiative response to the helpees' experiences as follows:

High initiative — Implementing steps

Moderate initiative — Defining goals and developing programs

Low initiative — Personalizing goals

As can be seen, the low levels of initiative are consistent with the high levels of personalizing (goal). The moderate levels of initiative involve defining goals and developing programs while the high levels involve implementing steps.

185

We can now complete our cumulative scale for helping. If the helper is attending, responding, personalizing and initiating the steps to achieve the operational goal, then the helper is operating at a fully-initiative level (level 5.0). If the helper is initiating only to define the goal, then the helper can be rated at an initiative level (level 4.5).

LEVELS OF HELPING

5.0   Initiating steps
4.5   Defining goals
4.0   Personalizing problem, feeling and goal
3.5   Personalizing meaning
3.0   Responding to meaning
2.5   Responding to feeling
2.0   Responding to content
1.5   Attending
1.0   Nonattending

LEVELS OF HELPING—ATTENDING, RESPONDING, PERSONALIZING AND INITIATING

Developing initiative is the culminating act in the helping process. Given personalized goals, initiating enables us to define the goals and develop the programs to achieve the goals. Resolving the helpees' problems and achieving their goals is what helping is all about.

Again, while the development of initiative is a mechanical process, it must also be an individualized process. We must constantly check back with the helpees' frames of references by making accurate responses to their experiences. At the highest levels of helping, responding and initiating are integrally related. There is no real understanding without action. There is no real action without understanding.

PHASES OF HELPING

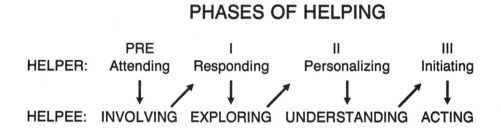

INVOLVING, EXPLORING, UNDERSTANDING AND ACTING

You now know about all of the basic helping skills: attending, responding, personalizing and initiating. You will need to work in a most intense and disciplined manner to learn to acquire and apply these skills. Practice until you can process these responses fluidly and effectively as part of your own helping personality. You might begin by making your own responses to the helpees in the following case study.

Case Study #8—Skilled Initiating

In a group of substance abusers are three men and one woman. Zeke is a 19-year-old college dropout who referred himself to treatment after an overdose of alcohol and tranquilizers that almost killed him. Frank is a 25-year-old who is in treatment as a condition of his probation for grand larceny. His drug of choice was cocaine. Lu Anne, who is usually called Muffin, is a 17-year-old chronic runaway who was referred to treatment by her parents after her last run. She has been a multiple drug user. Mitch is a 22-year-old college student who was referred to treatment by a friend. He stated he was having problems with "pot" and alcohol.

Lois, the helper, is an attractive woman in her midthirties. She has been a substance abuse counselor for the last five years. She has never had a problem with drugs or alcohol herself.

The room is set up with chairs and a chart pad in a circle. The room is bright and cheery. There are no antidrug or alcohol posters on the walls. There are several very good, dramatic water color portraits of people expressing intense emotions.

(This is an excerpt from the third counseling session. It starts about ten minutes into the session.)

Muffin: "Frank, you're looking irritated, with that scowl on your face."

Zeke: "Yeah, what's bothering you?"

Lois: "It sounds like some of the others have noticed it too."

Frank: "It's not anything I really want to talk about."

Muffin: "Okay, it's hard to open up, but that's one of the reasons why we're here; because we don't really communicate."

Frank: "Listen you little _____, when I want your advice I'll ask for it!"

Lois: "You're really torn up by what's bothering you. You're so angry you're lashing out at anyone."

Frank: "Hey, Muffin, I'm sorry...I just...I don't know."

Muffin: "Listen, I've been called worse. It's okay."

Lois: "You feel frightened because you aren't sure what we might say or do if you tell us what's concerning you."

Frank: "It's not that I don't trust you...It's just personal."

Zeke: "It is really hard to start opening up to people you hardly know."

Lois: "Frank, you're struggling with something that's really overwhelming and you don't want to lose control."

Frank: (silence, looking at the floor, trembling noticeably) "Yeah."

Lois: (gets up from her chair, squats down in front of Frank, and takes his hands) "You're in so much pain that you can hardly stand it." (Frank bursts into tears and hugs Lois. Muffin and Zeke, who are sitting next to Frank, each put a hand on his shoulder. Mitch sits watching, looking uncomfortable. After about a minute Frank starts to calm down. Lois hands him a kleenex.)

Frank: "I'm sorry. I've never done anything like that before. . .it's just. . ." (he blows his nose) "it hurts so bad."

Muffin: "So tell us what has you so torn to pieces."

Frank: "I've been dating this girl for the last few weeks. I realy like her. I thought we had something special going. Things were going fine, but then someone told her about my drug use and my record.

"Now, she doesn't want to see me again. She said that I had lied to her, that I didn't tell her the truth about myself. I wanted to tell her about what I've been through; I just didn't know how."

Zeke: "Wow!"

Lois: "You're really devastated by your girl friend confronting you and leaving you."

Frank: "Yeah, it really hurts. But the tough part is that I really have a difficult time meeting people. She was just about the only person outside this room I could talk to who isn't into drugs."

Muffin: "Yeah, I know what you mean. I don't have anyone either. I tried a couple of times, but no one wanted to have anything to do with me."

Lois: "Frank, you feel really frightened because of how lonely the world is for you. And Muffin, you sound really angry because you've tried to reach out and have been rejected."

Muffin: "At least when I was into drugs, sex and rock and roll, I wasn't so lonely."

Lois: "You feel humiliated because you think straight kids won't have anything to do with you."

Muffin: "Yeah, they all think I'm a whore. They won't have anything to do with me. I mean, at least when I did drugs I could shut off all this stuff. At least then I had friends."

Lois: "You're frightened because you don't think you'll be able to relate to another person without drugs."

Muffin: "I've messed up my life so bad I can't believe that anyone could like me. I mean I've done some sick, sick things when I've been high. Who'd want me?"

Lois: "You're terrified because you don't believe you can find any other way to be wanted."

Muffin: (tears on her cheeks) "I guess I'm not as tough as I thought."

Mitch: "Muffin? . . ." (She looks up. He reaches over to her hesitantly.) "I don't really know how to say this, but I think you're being too tough on yourself." (Muffin makes a hesitant smile.)

Lois: "You seem to be having the same feeling of hurt and fear of being alone, Mitch."

Mitch: (hesitantly) "Yeah, well . . ."

Zeke: "Boy, I sure can relate to what she's say-ing. I mean, I look back on my life and am so...ashamed! I just can't believe I can be any different. Who'd want to know a sleaze ball like me, you know?"

Lois: "You feel disgusted and ashamed, too. You don't know how to start fresh with people." (turning back to Mitch) "But, Mitch, I was hearing more pain, more yearning in your voice, rather than shame or disgust."

Mitch: "Yeah, I've been lonely and scared of peo-ple. I guess that's why I drank and smoked dope. It helped me feel powerful and in control, you know."

Lois: "So you feel frightened because you don't know how to relate to people either."

Mitch: "That's right."

Lois: "Frank, you feel hurt because you don't know if you can find someone to relate with. Muffin, you're scared that you'll never be able to experience real intimacy with someone. Mitch, you're frightened be-cause you're unsure how to start a relation-ship. And you, Zeke, are disappointed because you don't know if you can have a decent relationship." (multiple "Yeah" and "That's right.")

Muffin: "So what do we do?"

Lois: "Although your reasons are a little dif-ferent, it seems each of you is saying that you're frightened and hurt because you cannot find a way to make new friends and each of you wants to start fresh, healthy relationships.

(Lois looks at each person with an inquiring look. All nod their heads.)
"Or put another way, each of you is looking for a way to relate to other people without having to use drugs."

Mitch: "That's it exactly!" (multiple "Yeses" and "That's it!")

Lois: "Although each of you might have slightly different reasons for developing friendships, we need to start with learning how to relate."

Frank: "We really have to start at the beginning."

Lois: "Exactly. Each of you has to learn to relate to another person as yourself rather than the way you are when you're high."

Zeke: "But how will we know if we're relating right or not?"

Lois: "You're looking for a way to tell if you're relating properly or not."

Muffin: "That's easy. For me, it's if the person wants to see me again."

Frank: "For me, it's if the person shares something special with me."

Zeke: "I guess for me it's if the person enjoys being with me."

Lois: "You haven't said anything, Mitch."

Mitch: "I don't know. I guess it's the same as with Muffin."

Lois: "Okay, Zeke, Frank, it seems that if someone is willing to see you again, more than likely that person enjoys your company and will be willing to be self-disclosing with you."

Zeke: "Yeah, I guess."

Frank: "Sure."

Lois: "So we can use the willingness of the other person to interact with you again as an indication of how well you're relating."

Muffin: "That'll be a real trick. I can't even get them to talk to me the first time!"

Lois: "It's hard for you to even get an initial conversation started. Well, the very first thing we need to learn is how to greet people and get them involved with us. We also want to be able to size them up to see if we want them as friends."

Mitch: "I never know what to say."

Lois: "So learning how to do that makes sense for you. The next thing might be how to get them to talk about themselves."

Zeke: "Hey, yeah, if they think you're really interested in them they're more likely to become a friend."

Lois: "That's right. You're beginning to sound pleased with this. And the next step is getting them to want to intensify the relationship."

Muffin: "Can we really do this?"

Lois: "You're pretty surprised that learning how to make new friends is possible."

Muffin: "Hey, I thought I'd never be able to fit in with anyone but the freaks."

Lois: "You're feeling relieved because now there seems to be some hope"

Muffin: "When can we get started?"

Lois: "You want to get going right now" (Zeke and Frank simultaneously, "Yeah!") "Okay. First we'll learn how to decide on who we want as new friends. Then we'll learn how to get them to talk about themselves. And finally we'll learn how to intensify a relationship."

Mitch: "You really can teach us that?"

Lois: "You're questioning if I can deliver what I've said. And yet you sound hopeful."

Mitch: "Boy, I really want to learn."

Lois: "And I want to teach you. We'll start right now. We'll probably need the next three sessions to teach you the skills."

Zeke: "I'm really excited. Maybe I can change my life."

Lois: "You're really feeling relieved because you think you have a chance now."

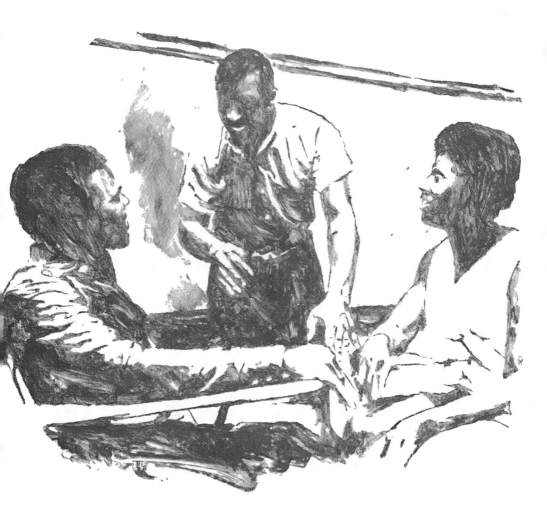

IV.
Summary

Our only reason to live is to grow. Human processing is our vehicle to growth. We humans are the products of our processing. Indeed, we are only human when we are processing. In the end, we either die growing or we die like animals, conditioned and impotent, homeless in our own world.

8.
RECYCLING THE HELPING PROCESS

This chapter addresses recycling the helping process. We will learn to facilitate more extensive exploration, more accurate understanding and more effective acting.

Here are some questions you can ask as you begin to think about recycling the helping process:

How do you know whether your action is effective?

How do you use the feedback you get?

How do you increase your effectiveness in life?

Read this case study. Based on your learnings see if you can find a reason why each helper response is an effective one.

Case Study #9—Skilled Helping

HELPEE INVOLVING/ HELPER ATTENDING		TYPE OF RESPONSE
Floyd:	"Man, I don't see how this jive is gonna get us anywhere! We've tried working together, but I don't see how we can."	
Helper:	"It's pretty frustrating to try working these things through without anyone's help. If you're free the next hour, I'd like to get together with you in my office."	Informing
Tom:	"It's O.K. with me, I guess."	
Helper:	"What about you, Floyd? I'd like to spend a little time getting to know both of you better. Then I'll be able to be more helpful."	Encouraging
Floyd:	"What about a cup of coffee instead?"	

Helper:	"Coffee's fine. I can really learn as much right here as in my office."	**Attending Contextually**
Floyd:	"What do you want to learn about us?"	
Tom:	"Yeah, I mean, I know you've been checking us out for quite a while."	
Helper:	"So you've been using your observing skills, too. You've noticed that I've really been paying attention to you."	**Attending Personally**
Tom:	"Uh huh. What have you been—you know—learning from us?"	
Helper:	"Well, I see two young guys who care enough about each other to stay in there fighting with each other. One's maybe more worn out than he should be and the other one's kind of edgy."	**Observing**
Floyd:	"You've really been using your eyes to see us, huh?"	
Helper:	". . . And my ears to hear, too."	**Listening**

HELPEE EXPLORING/ HELPER RESPONDING		**TYPE OF RESPONSE**
Floyd:	"The thing that really hassles me is the way you all act like everything's cool and I'm just supposed to relax and keep smiling!"	
Helper:	"You're saying it really gets to you when whites seem to want you to lay back and accept things."	**Responding to Content**
Tom:	"Man, we're all in this thing together! What's so special about you?"	

Helper: "You don't see why Floyd has to make a special case out of himself."

Responding to Content

Floyd: "You don't see it, huh Tom? Well maybe if you woke up black one morning a lot of things'd come clearer to you!"

Helper: "You feel really angry."

Responding to Feeling

Floyd: "Yeah, right! I mean, no white person can know what it's like to be black."

Helper: "You feel really furious when someone who isn't black tries to tell you how to act."

Responding to Meaning

Tom: "You got a lot of nerve to come on like that to me, man!"

Helper: "It makes you angry when Floyd doesn't seem to appreciate the way you act with him."

Responding to Meaning

Floyd: "Listen, you get treated like an individual. But me—either I get turned down flat, or else everyone wants to get alongside of my blackness without ever checking out who I really am on the inside."

Helper: "It burns you up that people never seem to get past your skin to what's underneath."

Responding to Meaning

Floyd: "Damn straight! I could be a genius or a flat-out fool and it still wouldn't matter as much as the fact that I'm black!"

Helper:	"It drives you wild because people just see how you look without ever caring what you do or how you feel."	**Responding to Meaning**
Tom:	"Listen, you're doing the same thing when you lump me in with every other white!"	
Helper:	"You feel angry and frustrated because Floyd doesn't see the ways you try to relate to him as an individual."	**Responding to Meaning**
Floyd:	"It's not the same thing, man. It's not like being black."	

HELPEE UNDERSTANDING/ HELPER PERSONALIZING		TYPE OF RESPONSE
Floyd:	"Dig it! They don't know who I am and they really aren't open to finding out."	
Helper:	"It really gets you down because you're not seen as a real person."	**Personalizing Meaning**
Tom:	"I'm trying—I really am, but for him I'm just another 'whitey.'"	
Helper:	"You're frustrated because you're just another white."	**Personalizing Meaning**
Floyd:	"Listen! It's a real drag—like having to run 10 miles just to warm up for a 100-yard dash. Like—well, take writing, for one. I tried to get on the board at the Lit. Magazine. But once they found out I wasn't into writing heavy race-type stuff, they weren't interested."	

Helper:	"It's infuriating because you can't find a way to get people to treat you like an individual in your own right."	**Personalizing Problems**
Tom:	"I feel the same way, man. If I could just convince you I really do see you as a person and not just a black."	
Helper:	"Tom, you get bummed out because you don't feel like a real person when Floyd sees you as just another white."	**Personalizing Problems**
Floyd:	"If I could just get through to people."	
Helper:	"You feel helpless because you can't get other people—especially Tom—to see you the way you really are."	**Personalizing Feelings**
Tom:	"In a way I'm in the same boat. Maybe I don't feel it as strongly as if I were black but it seems like the same thing to me."	
Helper:	"You feel like you're in the same boat—discouraged because you can't get the real you across to Floyd."	**Personalizing Feelings**
Floyd:	"I've got a lot to offer. I mean really, I'm into a lot of good things I'd like to share. Like—well, like my writing."	
Helper:	"Floyd, you feel miserable because you can't get other people to see what you really have to offer and you want to very badly."	**Personalizing Goals**

Tom:	"Listen, Floyd, there's nothing I'd like more than for you and me to get beyond this lame race stuff. I'd like for you to trust me and share with me."	
Helper:	"And Tom, you feel pretty low because you can't get Floyd to understand you and you really want to get him to see beyond your whiteness."	**Personalizing Goals**

HELPEE ACTING/ HELPER INITIATING

TYPE OF RESPONSE

Helper:	"So Floyd, you want other people to see you as an individual. And Tom, you want Floyd to see you as an individual. How could you each tell if you were reaching those goals?"	**Defining the Goals**
Floyd:	"A good indication for me would be if I could get on the board of the Literary Magazine without having to be the 'racial reporter.' "	
Tom:	"I'd just like to get rid of all my behaviors that Floyd feels are racist, so we can get beyond the color of our skins."	
Helper:	"O.K. Those sound like pretty realistic goals. Floyd, your first step might be to make a list of real contributions you feel you could make to the magazine's operation. And Tom, your first step might be to ask Floyd what the things are that you do which he feels are basically racist."	**Initiating First Step**

Floyd: "Hmm! That sounds O.K."

Tom: "Hey, I'm ready if you are."

Helper: "Tom, your next step could be to work with Floyd to prioritize which particular behaviors you should try to eliminate first. And Floyd, yours could be to find out what specific things a person has to do to be elected to the board."

Initiating Intermediate Steps

Tom: "I got you."

Floyd: "Yeah, you're making a whole lot of sense."

Helper: "When do you think you could be done with these beginning steps?"

Initiating Schedules

Floyd: "I can be done in a day or two."

Tom: "If Floyd has time, I could work on it tonight and tomorrow night."

Helper: "O.K. You might also decide to reward yourself for completing a step by doing something you really enjoy doing. If you fail to take the step, you don't get the reward."

Initiating Reinforcements

Floyd: "That's O.K. with me."

Tom: "Wow, the way you lay it all out it seems so easy! I can handle that for sure!"

Helper: "You feel a lot more hopeful because you begin to see how you can actually get where you want to go."

Responding to Meaning

Recycling Helping

Recycling is the ongoing processing that produces more and more effective acting. Developing more effective responses is the means by which we grow. Our future growth and development lies in recycling our helping and processing skills. We may use these helping skills with ourselves as well as with others. They will serve to facilitate our own processing.

Clearly, the core of the recycling skills are the processing skills we have already learned: exploring, understanding and acting. With the feedback that we receive from the environment for our previous action, we recycle the helping process: responding to facilitate exploring more extensively; personalizing to facilitate understanding more accurately; and initiating to facilitate acting more effectively.

RECYCLE HELPING

Recycle Action

Recycle Understanding

Recycle Exploration

RECYCLING HELPING

Recycling Exploration

Recycling exploration implies attempting to respond to achieve more extensive exploration of the helpees' experiences. For example, in implementing the running program, we may receive some time or distance feedback that causes us to re-explore our fitness programs. The feedback may cause us to explore other dimensions of running or other means of becoming fit.

In the interpersonal skills program, our helpee may explore alternate ways of responding to others or he may move on to consider other areas of his life where he might apply his responding skills. In recycling exploration, we are simply using the feedback to stimulate more extensive exploring about going back, moving on or modifying steps in our original program.

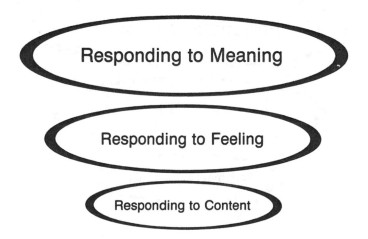

RECYCLING EXPLORATION

Recycling Understanding

Similarly, recycling understanding implies attempting to achieve a more accurate understanding of the helpees' goals by further personalizing the helpees' experiences. For example, in the running program the recycling of exploration may cause us to personalize new time and distance or fitness goals.

   In the interpersonal skills program, our helpee may set new goals in responding or move on to new goals in other skill areas. In recycling understanding, we are simply using the new base of exploring to develop new goals for acting.

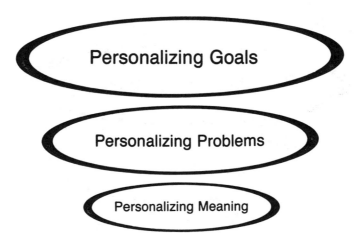

RECYCLING UNDERSTANDING

Recycling Action

Finally, recycling action implies initiating more effective action programs to achieve the new goals. For example, in the running program the new goals may cause us to develop new programs to achieve the goals.

In the interpersonal skills program, our helpee may develop new steps in learning to respond or move on to developing or implementing new steps to achieve the new goals. In recycling acting, we are simply using our understanding of new goals to develop new action programs to achieve those goals. We then go on to recycle again the feedback from our actions. The cycle of processing is the cycle of learning in life.

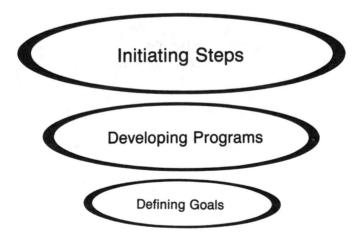

RECYCLING ACTION

Summary

We may want to conceptualize the helping process in terms that will remain with us: attending, responding, personalizing and initiating. If we know how each of these helping skills relates to the phases of human processing, then we will never be lost in anything we do in life. Indeed, the critical incidents that are now crises for us become simply opportunities for recycling our skills.

LEVELS OF HELPING

5.0	Initiating
4.0	Personalizing
3.0	Responding
2.0	Attending
1.0	Nonattending

Going through the helping process once with a helpee
may be an intense and fulfilling experience. But growth
is not static. Growth is life-long processing. A growing
person is constantly involved in processing in an ongoing, ever expanding spiral of life. This spiral emphasizes our purposeful effort to constantly improve our
functioning and our contributions to the world.

PHASES OF HELPING

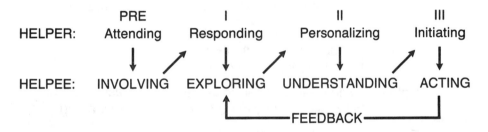

RECYCLING

You now know about recycling the helping process. You will want to practice these skills throughout your life in all living, learning and working situations.

Case Study #10—Skilled Helping

HELPEE PROCESSING/ HELPER RECYCLING	TYPE OF RESPONSE
Tom: "You know, I've tried to work things out with my parents. But things didn't work out the way I rehearsed them."	
Helper: "You're pretty upset because your rehearsals didn't pan out."	**Responding to Meaning**
Tom: "Yeah. Maybe I didn't check myself out while I was attending to them but I was really trying."	
Helper: "You're also upset because you left out a few key check steps."	**Responding to Meaning**
Tom: "Yeah. But I'm most disappointed in their reactions to me. I was really trying to attend to them. And they kept holding me off."	
Helper: "You're disappointed that they didn't receive your attentiveness."	**Responding to Meaning**
Tom: "Maybe they're just not ready for it. Or suspicious of it."	
Helper: "You're unsure because they may think you're only attentive to set them up for something bigger."	**Responding to Meaning**
Tom: "It's true. I often did set them up in the past. Maybe they're just not ready for a change in me."	

Helper:	"You're really sad because you're left out of their lives."	**Personalizing Meaning**
Tom:	"Maybe I'm not ready yet."	
Helper:	"You're really disappointed in yourself because you didn't bring it off with them."	**Personalizing the Problem**
Tom:	"They do mean so much to me."	
Helper:	"You're committed to working things through with them."	**Personalizing the Goal**
Tom:	"Yeah. I've revised my program and built in some more check steps. I'm going to make it work."	
Helper:	"You're determined to follow through with them. Maybe we need to work on a step that lets them know that you're really trying to change—to help them become attentive with you."	**Initiating a Program Step**
Tom:	"I just wish my parents could get into some listening instead of just yelling at me all the time."	
Helper:	"You're saying that your parents holler a lot and don't pay much attention to what you have to say."	**Responding to Content**
Joan:	"His parents and mine, too. Honestly, they treat us like we were little kids!"	
Helper:	"You feel pretty angry with them."	**Responding to Feeling**

Tom:	"They're living in a dream world."	
Helper:	"It bugs you that they're so out of touch."	**Responding to Meaining**
Joan:	"They don't even know that the real world today is a whole new thing!"	
Helper:	"You feel mad because they don't even know what's going on."	**Responding to Meaning**
Tom:	"I just wish they'd let up on us."	
Helper:	"You really resent that they're always on your back."	**Responding to Meaning**
Joan:	"We both do. See, we've been making some plans of our own. Only they won't believe that we're—I don't know—mature enough to handle things."	
Helper:	"It's frustrating when your parents don't accept your capability."	**Responding to Meaning**
Tom:	"You know it! I mean, all we want to do is live together. That's no big thing today, right? But they act like such jerks, they think we're going to ruin our lives!"	
Helper:	"You feel furious because they won't let you make your own decisions."	**Responding to Meaning**
Joan:	"Exactly! We've tried to be responsible with them, but it hasn't helped. I don't know how we're supposed to convince them that we're well, practically adults."	

Helper: "What it comes down to is that
you are both fed up with the
fact that they want to keep you
on a leash and you want to live
your own lives on your own   **Responding**
terms and not theirs."   **to Meaning**

Tom: "It's really a messed-up situation any way you look at it."

Helper: "It's a lousy feeling because
even though you're pretty mad
at your parents, you still care a   **Personalizing**
lot about how they feel."   **Meaning**

Joan: "I—yeah, I've though about that."

Tom: "Well, I guess I've probably had
some questions myself. I mean,
how could we help it when our
parents are making us look at
the bad side all the time?"

Helper: "So you're kind of uneasy, too,
Tom, because you're not confident enough in yourself to be
sure you are doing the right   **Personalizing**
thing."   **Meaning**

Joan: "It's like—well, when my
parents tell me what to do, it
makes me very defensive. But
when I'm alone—I don't
know—what if we went ahead
and then found out we were
making a mistake?"

Helper: "It concerns you because you
can't figure out for sure what's
the best thing for you both to
do regardless of what others   **Personalizing**
want you to do."   **the Problem**

Tom:	"Un huh. I mean—well, I love Joan too much to want to do something for the wrong reason—just to get back at my parents, for example."	
Helper:	"It's scary because you can't be sure you're doing the right thing for the right reasons."	**Personalizing the Feeling**
Joan:	"That's just it. I don't think we would even be so ready to live together if our parents weren't so set against it."	
Helper:	"You feel frightened because you can't stop living in reaction to your parents even though you want to make decisions that reflect who you are."	**Personalizing the Goal**
Tom:	"Yeah, we've got to be ourselves."	
Helper:	"You're certain you want to be yourselves even though you're sometimes not sure what that really means."	**Responding to Meaning**
Helper:	"It sounds to me like your goal isn't really to live together—but that you really want to find a way to make decisions based on your own values, rather than just reacting to others. That really means being able to use your personal values to decide whether or not to live together."	**Defining the Goal**
Tom:	"Yeah—but that's just it. Even when I know something is	

important, I can't seem to figure out what to do about it.''

Helper: "It's irritating when you can't figure out how to live by your own values. The first thing you might do is explore your values and then make a list of all the things that are important to you."

Initiating the
First Step

Joan: "Sure—but how's that going to help us know what to do?"

Helper: "Well, once you know what's important, you can prioritize your values by deciding which one is most important, next important, and so on—then you can use all this information to make the decision."

Initiating
Intermediate
Steps

Tom: "I get it—you mean some of our values ought to influence our decision more than others and we have to know that to make the best choice."

Helper: "That's right. When do you think you could make up a list of your values and priorities so we could get together again and talk them over?"

Initiating
Schedules

Joan: "We can get that done this afternoon and tonight."

Helper: "O.K. If you do that, then I'll meet with you both again on Thursday to review what you've done and to show you how to use those values systematically to make the best choices for you." — **Initiating Reinforcements**

Tom: "I think we're going to feel a whole lot better once we've worked this thing through."

Helper: "You already feel a lot better just knowing that you're going to be able to make the best decision based on the things that are really important to you." — **Responding to Meaning**

9.
DEVELOPING HUMAN RESOURCES

The real purpose of helping is human resource development or HRD. The helpers employ helping skills in order
to facilitate their helpees' HRD. In order to facilitate
HRD, the helpers must themselves develop their own
resources.

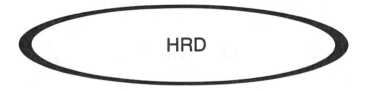

HELPING → HRD

The basic areas of HRD include physical, emotional and intellectual dimensions. The physical area emphasizes fitness. The emotional area emphasizes motivation. The intellectual area emphasizes thinking.

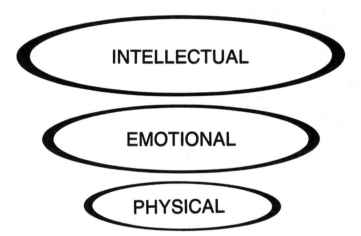

AREAS OF HRD

Levels of Physical Fitness

Just as we have learned and measured interpersonal skills, so may we learn and measure physical fitness skills. At the lowest levels, people are sick or just barely surviving. At the highest levels, people function with intensity and stamina. At minimally effective levels, people only have the energy sufficient to adapt to daily requirements. Physical fitness provides the energy base from which we draw the strength needed to reach higher levels of emotional and intellectual functioning.

LEVELS OF FITNESS

5	STAMINA
4	INTENSITY
3	ADAPTABILITY
2	SURVIVAL
1	SICKNESS

PHYSICAL FITNESS → ENERGY

Levels of Emotional Motivation

In a similar manner, we can learn and measure levels of emotional motivation. At the lowest levels, people are unmotivated or respond only to incentives. At the highest levels, people are motivated to fulfill themselves and are committed to a mission outside of themselves. At minimally effective levels, people internalize their motivation to achieve or perform at levels of excellence. Motivation is the catalyst for using our intellects.

LEVELS OF MOTIVATION

5   MISSION
4   SELF-FULFILLMENT
3   ACHIEVEMENT
2   INCENTIVES
1   UNMOTIVATED

MOTIVATION → CATALYST

Levels of Intellectual Processing

Likewise, we can learn and measure levels of intellectual processing or thinking. At the lowest levels, people are unprepared or minimally involved in thinking. At higher levels, people can explore by analyzing their experience, understand by defining objectives and act by developing and implementing programs. Using our intellects fully enables us to actualize our humanity.

LEVELS OF THINKING

5   ACTING
4   UNDERSTANDING
3   EXPLORING
2   INVOLVED
1   UNPREPARED

THINKING ⟶ ACTUALIZING

Levels of Human Resource Development

We may generalize the levels of physical, emotional and intellectual functioning in the levels of HRD. At the lower levels, we are detractors or at best observers of life. At the higher levels, we not only participate and contribute but also demonstrate leadership and initiative in maintaining life wherever and whenever we find it. This is what enables us to be helpers. This is also what enables helpees to be transformed into helpers.

LEVELS OF HRD

5 LEADER
4 CONTRIBUTOR
3 PARTICIPANT
2 OBSERVER
1 DETRACTOR

LEVELS OF HRD

LEVELS OF HRD

		PHYSICAL FITNESS	EMOTIONAL MOTIVATION	INTELLECTUAL PROCESSING
LEADER	5.0	Stamina	Mission	Acting
CONTRIBUTOR	4.0	Intensity	Self-fulfillment	Understanding
PARTICIPANT	3.0	Adaptability	Achievement	Exploring
OBSERVER	2.0	Survival	Incentives	Involved
DETRACTOR	1.0	Sickness	Unmotivated	Unprepared

Summary

We may summarize the critical ingredients of HRD in a formula. As may be seen, physical fitness (P) is the energizer, emotional motivation (E) is the catalyzer and intellectual thinking (I) is the actualizer. As may be noted, HRD is a function of our physical fitness × our emotional motivation × our intellectual processing—thinking $[HRD = f(P \cdot E^2 \cdot I^3)]$. As may also be noted, the real power of HRD lies in the power of human processing or thinking.

$$HRD = P \cdot E^2 \cdot I^3$$

$$HRD = P \cdot E^2 \cdot I^3$$

The Age of Information imposes tremendous "information press" upon all people. The kinds of problems that people bring to helping will be increasingly situationally determined—changing schools, losing jobs, starting over. The kinds of material that helpers deal with will be increasingly information-based. Indeed, helpees as well as helpers will need to learn these intellectual and informational processing skills. The power of helping lies in these intellectual processing skills along with the interpersonal processing skills we have already learned.

HELPING IN TRANSITION

Just as the ingredients of helping are expanding, then, so are the requirements for the helpers. In order to develop the human resources of others through helping, helpers must first develop their own resources. First and foremost among the new ingredients for helpers are the intellectual or informational processing skills. Along with interpersonal processing skills, the intellectual processing skills are the major source of personal power in the helpers.

HELPERS IN TRANSITION

In conclusion, skills are the vehicles by which we
facilitate HRD. We may help ourselves as well as others.
Indeed, at the highest levels, we must help ourselves to
develop our resources before we can help others to
develop their resources. The purpose of helping is
human growth. Indeed, the purpose of life is to grow.
Therefore growth is worth any price—even skilling
ourselves in order to help skill others.

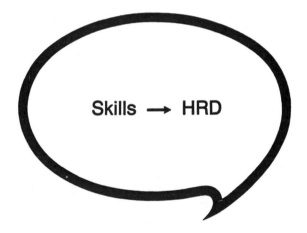

SKILLS → HRD

Appendices

APPENDIX A

FEELING WORD LIST

Happy	Sad	Angry	Confused
alive	awful	agitated	anxious
amused	bad	annoyed	awkward
anxious	blue	bitter	baffled
calm	bummed out	burned up	bewildered
cheerful	crushed	critical	bothered
content	depressed	disgusted	crazy
delighted	desperate	dismayed	dazed
ecstatic	devastated	enraged	disorganized
elated	disappointed	envious	disoriented
energized	dissatisfied	fed up	distracted
excited	distressed	frustrated	disturbed
fantastic	disturbed	furious	embarrassed
fortunate	down	hostile	frustrated
friendly	embarrassed	impatient	helpless
fulfilled	gloomy	irate	hopeless
glad	glum	irritated	jolted
good	hateful	livid	lost
great	hopeless	mad	mixed up
hopeful	hurt	outraged	panicky
lively	lonely	perturbed	paralyzed
loving	lost	put out	perplexed
motherly	low	riled	puzzled
optimistic	miserable	resentful	shocked
overjoyed	painful	seething	stuck
peaceful	sorry	sore	stunned
pleased	terrible	ticked off	surprised
proud	turned off	uptight	tangled
refreshed	uneasy	worked up	trapped
relaxed	unhappy		troubled
relieved	unloved		uncertain
rested	upset		uncomfortable
satisfied			undecided
spirited			unsure
thankful			upset
thrilled			weak
turned on			
up			
warm			
wonderful			

234

Scared

afraid
anxious
apprehensive
awed
cautious
chicken
edgy
fearful
frightened
hesitant
horrified
insecure
intimidated
jumpy
lonely
nervous
panicky(ed)
shaky
tense
terrified
threatened
timid
uneasy
unsure
worried

Weak

ashamed
blocked
bored
defenseless
demoralized
disorganized
distracted
discouraged
embarrassed
exhausted
fragile
frail
frustrated
guilty
helpless
horrible
ill
impotent
inadequate
incapable
insecure
lifeless
lost
overwhelmed
powerless
quiet
run-down
shaky
shy
sick
small
stressed
stupid
timid
tired
unsure
useless
vulnerable
worn out

Strong

active
aggressive
alert
angry
bold
brave
capable
confident
determined
eager
energetic
happy
healthy
intense
loving
mean
open
positive
potent
powerful
quick
secure
solid
spirited
super
sure
tough

APPENDIX B

THE HELPING MODEL

The research of helping skills demonstrations over the last two decades is summarized in Tables 1 and 2. As can be seen in Table 1, 164 studies of 158,940 recipients are involved. The studies are divided as to their sources of effect—the effects of trained helpers or the effects of training helpees directly. In turn, the effects upon helpees are demonstrated in living, learning and working areas of functioning.

TABLE 1.

An Index of Tables for the Studies of Recipient Living, Learning and Working Outcomes*

SOURCES OF EFFECT

Outcome Areas	Helpers	Helpees
Living	Table 2 (22 Studies) 25,682 Helpees	Table 6 (35 Studies) 2,279 Helpees
Learning	Tables 3 & 4 (32 Studies) 81,298 Learners	Table 7 (26 Studies) 3,610 Learners
Working	Table 5 (22 Studies) 33,836 Employees	Table 8 (27 Studies) 12,235 Employees
Sub-Totals	(76 Studies) 140,816 Recipients	(88 Studies) 18,124 Recipients
Grand Total	(164 Studies) 158,940 Recipients	

*(Carkhuff, 1983)

TABLE 2.

A Summary Index of Percentages of Predominantly
Positive Results of IPS Studies and Indices of Helpee
Living, Learning, and Working Outcomes*

OUTCOMES	HELPERS	HELPEES	
LIVING (Table 2)			(Table 6)
Studies (N = 22)	91% Positive	91% Positive	Studies (N = 35)
Indices (N = 114)	83% Positive	85% Positive	Indices (N = 128)
LEARNING (Tables 3 & 4)			(Table 7)
Studies (N = 32)	97% Positive	100% Positive	Studies (N = 26)
Indices (N = 261)	92% Positive	99% Positive	Indices (N = 78)
WORKING (Table 5)			(Table 8)
Studies (N = 22)	100% Positive	100% Positive	Studies (N = 27)
Indices (N = 81)	96% Positive	98% Positive	Indices (N = 107)
SUB-TOTAL			
Studies (N = 76)	96% Positive	96% Positive	Studies (N = 88)
Indices (N = 456)	92% Positive	92% Positive	Indices (N = 313)
GRAND TOTAL			
Studies (N = 164)	96% Positive		
Indices (N = 769)	92% Positive		

*(Carkhuff, 1983)

As can be seen in Table 2, the studies of the effects of helpers upon helpees are 96 percent positive while the indices are 92 percent positive. This means that various helpers—parents, counselors, teachers, employers—have constructive effects upon their helpees—children, counselees, students, employees—when trained in interpersonally-based helping skills. As can also be seen in Table 2, the studies of the direct effects of training the helpees are also 96 percent positive while the indices are 92 percent positive. This means that trained helpees—children, counselees, students, employees—demonstrate constructive change or gain when trained in interpersonally-based self-helping skills.

Overall, the studies of the effects of both helpers and direct training upon helpees are 96 percent positive while the indices are 92 percent positive. This means that our chances of achieving any reasonable living, learning or working outcome are about 95 percent when either helpers or helpees are training in interpersonally-based helping skills. Conversely, the chances of achieving any human goal without trained helpers or helpees are random.

Together, the results of these studies constitute an answer to the challenges to the efficacy of the helping professions (Anthony, 1979; Eysench, 1960, 1965; Levitt, 1963; Lewis, 1965).

NATURALISTIC STUDIES

One answer to the challenges to helping came from studying the natural variability of the professionally-treated groups. The clients and patients of professional helpers demonstrated a greater range of effects than those in professionally "untreated" groups (Rogers et al., 1967; Traux and Carkhuff, 1967). This meant that professional practitioners tended to have a greater spread of effects on their patients; some got significantly better and some got worse. This finding suggested one very consoling conclusion: counseling and psychotherapy really did make a difference. It also suggested one very distressing conclusion: counseling and psychotherapy have a two-edged effect—they may be helpful or harmful (Bergin and Garfield, 1971).

Furthermore, the truly significant finding was that you could account, at least in part, for these helpful, neutral and harmful effects. The effects could be determined by the levels of functioning of the helpers on certain interpersonal dimensions such as empathy or empathic understanding. Counselors and therapists who offered high levels of a certain core of interpersonal dimensions facilitated the process and outcome of their clients and patients while clients and patients of helpers offering low levels of understanding stayed the same or were retarded in their process and outcome (Rogers et al., 1967; Truax and Carkhuff, 1967).

PREDICTIVE STUDIES

Following these early naturalistic studies, a number of predictive validity studies were conducted. These involved manipulating the levels of the helper's functioning on interpersonal dimensions such as empathy. The effects of these manipulations were studied both within the helping process and upon the helping outcomes. In general, within the helping process, the helpees (clients and patients) changed according to the helper's level of functioning: when the helpers offered high levels of interpersonal dimensions such as empathy, the helpees explored their problems in meaningful ways. When the helpers offered low levels of interpersonal dimensions, the helpees did not explore their problems in meaningful ways (Carkhuff and Alexik, 1967; Holder et al., 1967; Piaget et al., 1968; Truax and Carkhuff, 1967).

In the studies of helping outcomes, it was found that the helpees moved in the direction of the helpers' levels of functioning. In general, helpees of helpers functioning at high levels of these interpersonal dimensions moved toward higher levels of functioning. Helpees of helpers functioning at low levels of these interpersonal dimensions moved toward lower levels of functioning (Pagell, et al., 1967).

GENERALIZATION STUDIES

The next series of studies sought to generalize the effects of these interpersonal dimensions to other helping and human relationships. The first effort was to study the effects of teachers' levels of interpersonal functioning upon learners' development. Aspy and Roebuck (1972) divided teachers into high and low levels of interpersonal functioning and found significant relationships with student achievement indices such as Word Meaning, Paragraph Meaning, Spelling, Word Study Skills and Language. A number of subsequent studies were conducted assessing the relationship of interpersonal dimensions with a variety of other student outcome indices: the students of teachers offering high levels of these interpersonal dimensions demonstrated significant constructive gains in areas of emotional, interpersonal, and intellectual functioning (Aspy and Roebuck, 1977).

These effects have been generalized in all areas of helping and human relationships where the "more knowing" person influences the "less knowing" person: parent-child relations (Carkhuff, 1971a, 1983b; Carkhuff and Pierce, 1976); teacher-student relations (Aspy and Roebuck, 1977; Carkhuff, 1969, 1983a); counselor-client relations (Berenson and Carkhuff, 1967; Carkhuff and Berenson, 1967, 1977); and therapist-patient relations (Anthony, 1979; Rogers et al., 1967; Truax and Carkhuff, 1967). In general, the "less knowing" persons will move toward the levels of functioning of the "more knowing" persons over time, depending on both the extensiveness and intensity of contacts: helpers of high-level functioning helpers get better on a variety of process and outcome indices, while helpees of low-level functioning helpers get worse.

EXTENSION STUDIES

Finally, a number of studies were conducted to extend the dimensions of helping. For example, Vitalo (1970) found that the effects of behavior modification programs were contingent, in part, upon the modifiers' levels of interpersonal functioning. Michelson and Stevic (1971) found that career information-seeking behavior was dependent upon the helpers' levels of interpersonal functioning in interaction with their reinforcement programs. In general, those helpers who functioned at the highest levels, and had the most systematic helping programs, were most effective in helping their helpees.

Simultaneously, the core interpersonal dimensions were gradually extended and then factored into responsive and initiative dimensions (Berenson and Mitchell, 1974; Carkhuff, 1969, 1983a). (Responsive dimensions respond to the helpee's experience. Initiative dimensions, while taking into consideration the helpee's experience, are generated from the helpers' experience.) In addition, a number of systematic helping programs were developed to extend the helper's initiative activities to culminate in effective action programs for the helpees (Carkhuff, 1969, 1983a; 1971a, 1983b).

In summary, those helping dimensions that appear naturally in a limited number of effective helpers were validated in predictive studies of both helping process and outcome. In addition, the effectiveness of these helping dimensions was generalized to all helping and human relationships. Finally, these dimensions were extended to equip the helpers with more of the ingredients they needed to effectively help others. The acceptance of these fundamental ingredients of helping has been widely demonstrated in the professional literature (Brammer, 1979; Combs et al., 1978; Danish and Hauer, 1973; Egan, 1975; Gazda, 1973; Gordon, 1975; Hackney and Cormier, 1979; Johnson, 1972; Okun, 1976; Patterson, 1973).

THE EVOLUTION OF THE DIMENSIONS

Over a period of time, the core dimensions of helping have evolved and have been extended in a never-ending attempt to account for helping effectiveness. What began with a gross definition of the dimension of empathy, has evolved into an extensive equation for human resource development. In order to understand these dimensions, we must understand four things: the sources of helping dimensions as well as their evolution; the helping process which these dimensions impact; the helper skills which operationalize the dimensions; and the helpee outcomes which these dimensions are intended to achieve.

HELPER SOURCES

There are two fundamental approaches to helping. One may be called the insight approach. The other may be conceived of as the action approach. The insight approach has been supported by many traditional therapeutic schools. In particular, the psychoanalytic, neoanalytic and client-centered practioners have emphasized the client's insight as the basis for the development of an effective set of assumptions about his or her world (Adler, 1927; Freud, 1933; Fromm, 1947; Horney, 1945; Jung, 1939; Rank, 1929; Rogers et al., 1967; Sullivan, 1938). The action approach has been promulgated by the learning theory and behavior modification schools as well as the trait-and-factor school, which matches people to jobs and vice versa. These schools have emphasized the client's development and implementation of rational action plans for managing his or her world (Eysenck, 1960; Ginzberg et al., 1951; Krasner and Ullman, 1965; Parsons, 1909; Super, 1949; Watson, 1916; Wolpe et al., 1964).

Unfortunately, both the insight and action approaches are incomplete without the other. Most insight approaches fail to develop the insights programmatically so that the client can "own" them. Even when they do, they fail to systematically develop action programs flowing from these insights. Similarly, while the action approaches develop their programs effectively, they fail to consolidate whatever behavior changes thay have accomplished. They neglect to complement the action with insights so that the client can guide his or her own life (Carkhuff and Berenson, 1976; 1967, 1977). In order to effectively help human beings to change behavior, the insight and action approaches must be integrated into one effective helping process.

HELPING PROCESS

In order to demonstrate a change or gain in behavior, the helpees must act differently from the way they did before. In order to act effectively, the helpees must have insights or understand accurately their goals, and the ways to achieve them. In order to understand their goals, the helpees must explore their world experientially. These three learning or relearning processes are the phases of helping through which the helpees must be guided (Carkhuff and Berenson, 1976).

The helpees must first explore where they are in relation to their worlds and the significant people in their worlds. They must next understand where they are in relation to where they want to be. Finally, they must act to get from where they are to where they want to be. With the feedback from their action, they can recycle the learning process for more extensive exploration, more accurate understanding and more effective action (Carkhuff and Berenson, 1976).

HELPER SKILLS

In order to be effective in helping, then, the helper skills must facilitate the helpee's movement through the three-way helping process. The historic dimension of empathy was complemented by unconditional positive regard and genuineness (Rogers et al., 1967). These dimensions were transformed by more operational definitions into accurate empathy, respect and genuineness (Carkhuff, 1969, 1983a; Truax and Carkhuff, 1967). They were, in turn, complemented by other dimensions including specificity or concreteness, self-disclosure, confrontation, and immediacy and then factored into responsive and initiative dimensions (Berenson and Mitchell, 1974; Carkhuff, 1969, 1983a).

The responsive dimensions (empathy, respect, specificity of expression) responded to the helpee's experience and, thus, facilitated the helpee's movement toward understanding. The initiative dimensions (genuineness, self-disclosure, confrontation, immediacy and concreteness) were generated from the helper's experience and stimulated the helpee's movement toward action (Berenson and Mitchell, 1974; Carkhuff, 1971a, 1983b). These initiative dimensions were later extended to incorporate the problem-solving skills and program development skills needed to fully help the helpees to achieve appropriate outcomes (Carkhuff, 1985a, 1985b; Carkhuff and Anthony, 1979).

HELPEE OUTCOMES

In the early research, the helpee outcomes emphasized the emotional changes or gains of the helpees. Since the helping methods were insight-oriented, the process emphasized helpee exploration, and the outcome assessments measured the changes in the helpee's level of emotional insights (Rogers et al., 1967; Truax and Carkhuff, 1967). Clearly, these emotional outcomes were restrictive because they were assessing only one dimension of the helpee's functioning.

These outcomes were later defined more broadly to incorporate all dimensions of human resource development to which the helping process is dedicated. The emotional dimension was extended to incorporate the interpersonal functioning of the helpees (Carkhuff, 1969, 1983a; 1971a, 1983b). The dimension of physical functioning was added to measure relevant data on the helpees' fitness and energy levels (Collingwood, 1972). The intellectual dimension was added to measure the helpees' intellectual achievement and capabilities (Aspy and Roebuck, 1972, 1977).

In summary, helping effectiveness is a function of the helper's skills to facilitate the helping process to accomplish helping outcomes. Helping outcomes include the physical, emotional and intellectual dimensions of human resource development. The helping process, by which outcomes are accomplished, emphasizes the helpee's exploration, understanding and acting. The helping skills, by which the process is facilitated, include responding and initiating skills.

THE HELPING SKILLS

The responsive and initiative factors of helping dominate the helping process. They facilitate the exploration, understanding and action that culminate in the physical, emotional and intellectual helpee outcomes. As a result of attempts to teach helpers how to accomplish these processes and outcomes, the responsive and initiative dimensions were further refined into concrete helping skills. These helping skills are called attending, responding, personalizing and initiating. The attending skills are preparatory to responding and the personalizing skills are transitional between responding and initiating.

ATTENDING SKILLS

Attending skills involve communicating a "hovering attentiveness" to the helpee. By attending physically, the helper communicates interest in the helpee's welfare. By observing and listening, the helper learns from and about the helpee. Attending is the richest source of learning about the helpee (Barker, 1971; Birdwhistell, 1967; Ekman et al., 1972; Garfield, 1971; Genther and Moughan, 1977; Genther and Sacuzzo, 1977; Hall, 1959, 1976; Ivey, 1971, 1978; Mehrabian, 1972; Schefflen, 1969; Smith-Hanen, 1977).

Within the helping process, attending serves to facilitate the helpee's involvement in helping. By communicating interest in the helpee, the helper establishes the conditions for the helpee's involvement in the helping process. Reduced to their minimum, attending skills may be seen as the acts of being decent to the helpee in a world that is very often indecent (Carkhuff and Berenson, 1976).

RESPONDING SKILLS

Basic responding skills involve the helper's accurate understanding of the helpee's experience. They include first discriminating and then communicating the content and feelings of the helpee's experience. When employed at levels interchangeable with the helpee's experience, they serve to insure that the helper is fully in tune with the helpee (Aspy and Roebuck, 1977; Carkhuff, 1969, 1983a; Carkhuff and Berenson, 1967, 1977; Rogers et al., 1967; Truax and Carkhuff, 1967).

Responding skills serve to stimulate the helpee's exploration of where he or she is in his or her experience of the world. The accurate response becomes a mirror image of the helpee's experience. Responding skills also serve to reinforce the helpee's exploration by showing the helpee that the helper is fully in tune with the helpee's experience (Carkhuff and Berenson, 1976).

PERSONALIZING SKILLS

Personalizing skills involve responding to the personal implications of the meaning, problem, feeling and, finally, the goal. The helper processes the learning from helpee exploration and initiates movement toward understanding through a consideration of personalized implications. Personalizing skills culminate in the helpee's personal experience of the problem as the inability to handle difficult situations (Adler, 1927; Anthony, 1971; Berenson and Mitchell, 1974; Binswanger, 1956; Carkhuff, 1969, 1983a; Carkhuff and Berenson, 1976; Freud, 1933; Fromm, 1947; Heidegger, 1962; Horney, 1945, Jung, 1939; May, 1961; Rank, 1929; Sullivan, 1948).

Personalizing skills are used to provide a transition from responding to initiating and from exploring to acting. When employed effectively, they facilitate the helpee's understanding of where he or she wants to be in the world. They serve to focus upon the helpee's goals which are the basis for acting (Carkhuff and Berenson, 1976).

INITIATING SKILLS

Finally, initiating skills involve operationalizing the goals, and then developing and implementing the steps to achieve these goals. Again, remember that the goals are calculated to resolve the helpee's problems. Most simply, initiative skills foster the development and implementation of the mechanical steps that are required to achieve the personalized goals that the helpee has developed (Authier et al., 1975; Carkhuff,

1969, 1971b, 1983a, 1985a, 1985b; Carkhuff and Anthony, 1979; Collingwood et al., 1978; Goldstein, 1976; Ivey, 1976; Sprinthall and Mosher, 1971).

The initiating skills conclude the first cycle of the helping process. The helper employs initiative skills to stimulate the helpee's acting to achieve his or her goals. When employed effectively, initiative skills facilitate the helpee's acting to get to where he or she wants to be in the world (Carkhuff and Berenson, 1976).

In summary: the attending skills serve to involve the helpee in helping; responding skills facilitate exploration; personalizing skills facilitate understanding; and initiating skills stimulate acting. Again, with the feedback from acting, the helping or learning process is recycled until the goals are achieved.

THE TRAINING APPLICATIONS

It was a natural step to train helpers in helping skills and study the effects on helping outcomes. Indeed, the development of both the skills technologies and the training systems was a highly interactional process, with each refining the other and both, in turn, being shaped by their outcomes. It was also only natural that the first of these training applications take place with credentialed counselors and therapists. Next came the training of lay and indigenous helper populations, followed by the direct training of helpee populations to service themselves.

CREDENTIALED HELPERS

The first series of training applications demonstrated that professional helpers could be trained to function at levels commensurate with "outstanding" practitioners (Truax & Carkhuff, 1967). In a later series, it was established that credentialed professionals could, in the brief time of 100 hours or less, learn to function above minimally effective and self-sustaining levels of interpersonal skills, levels beyond those offered by most "outstanding" practitioners (Carkhuff, 1969, 1983a). Perhaps most importantly, trained counselors were able to involve their counselees in the helping process at levels that led to constructive change or gain. In one demonstration study in guidance, against a very low base success rate of 13 to 25 percent, the trained counselors were able to demonstrate success rates between 74 and 91 percent (Carkhuff and Berenson, 1976).

A series of training applications in teaching soon followed. Hefele (1971) found student achievement to be a function of systematic training of teachers in helping skills. Berenson (1971) found the experimentally-trained teachers were rated significantly higher in interpersonal skills and competency in the classroom than were other teachers who received a variety of control conditions (including a training control group, a Hawthorne Effect control group and a control group proper). Aspy and Roebuck (1977), building upon their earlier work, have continued to employ a variety of teacher training strategies demonstrating the positive effects of helping skills upon student physical, emotional and intellectual functioning.

FUNCTIONAL PROFESSIONALS

It is clear that a dimension such as interpersonal functioning is not the exclusive province of credentialed professionals. Lay personnel can learn as well as professionals to be caring and empathic in their relations with helpee populations. With this growing recognition, a number of training applications using lay personnel were conducted. The majority of these programs dealt with staff personnel.

Staff personnel, such as nurses and hospital attendants, policemen and prison guards, dormitory counselors and community volunteers, were trained and their effects in treatment studied. The effects were very positive for both the staff and helpee populations for, after all, the line staff and helpee populations were those who lived most intimately with each other. In general, the lay helpers were able to elicit significant changes in work behaviors, discharge rates, recidivism rates and a variety of other areas including self-reports, significant-other-reports and expert-reports (Carkhuff, 1969, 1971a, 1983a, 1983b; Carkhuff and Berenson, 1976).

INDIGENOUS PERSONNEL

The difference between functional professional staff and indigenous functional professionals is the difference between the attendant and the patient, the policeman and the delinquent, the guard and the inmate, and the teacher and the student. That is to say, indigenous personnel are part of the community being serviced. It is a natural extension of the lay helper training principle to train helpee recipients as well as staff.

Here the research indicates that, with systematic selection and training, indigenous functional professionals can work effectively with the populations from which they are drawn. For example, human relations specialists drawn from recipient ranks have facilitated school and work adjustments for troubled populations. New careers teachers, themselves drawn from the ranks of the unemployed, have systematically helped others to learn the skills they needed in order to get and hold meaningful jobs (Carkhuff, 1971a, 1983b).

HELPEE POPULATIONS

The logical culmination of helper training is to train helpee populations directly in the kinds of skills which they need to service themselves. Thus, parents of emotionally disturbed children were systematically trained in the skills which they needed to function effectively with themselves and their children (Carkhuff and Bierman, 1970). Patients were trained to offer each other rewarding human relationships. The results were significantly more positive than all other forms of treatment, including individual or group therapy, drug treatment or "total push" treatment (Pierce and Drasgow, 1969). Training was, indeed, the preferred mode of treatment!

The concept of training as treatment led directly to the development of programs to train entire communities to create a therapeutic milieu. This has been accomplished most effectively in institutional-type settings where staff and residents are trained in the kinds of skills necessary to work effectively with each other. Thus both institutional and community-based criminal justice settings have yielded data indicating reduced recidivism and increased employability (Carkhuff, 1974; Collingwood et al., 1978; Montgomery and Brown, 1980).

In summary, both lay staff and indigenous personnel may be selected and trained as functional professional helpers. In these roles, they can effect any human resource development that professionals can—and more! Further, teaching the helpee populations the kinds of skills which they need to service themselves is a direct extension of the helper principle. When we train people in the skills which they need to function effectively in their worlds, we increase the probability that they will, in fact, begin to live, learn and work in increasingly constructive ways.

CONCLUSIONS

In summary, training in interpersonal skills-based helping programs significantly increases the chances of our being effective in improving indices of helpee living, learning or working. Simply stated, trained helpers effectively elicit and use the input and feedback from the helpees concerning their helping effectiveness. Similarly, trained helpees learn to deal up, down and sideways in developing their own goals and programs.

We have found that all helping and human relationships may be "for better or for worse." The effects depend upon the helper's level of skills in facilitating the helpee's movement through the helping process toward constructive helping outcomes. These responsive and initiative helping skills constitute the core of all helping experiences.

The helping skills may be used in all one-to-one and one-to-group relationships. They are used in conjunction with the helper's specialty skills in counseling, teaching and working. They may be used in conjunction with any of a number of potential preferred modes of treatment, drawn from a variety of helping orientations, to meet the helpee's needs. Finally, the same skills may be taught directly to the helpees in order to help them help themselves: teaching clients skills is the preferred mode of treatment for most helpee populations.

In conclusion, the helping skills will enable us to have helpful rather than harmful effects upon the people with whom we relate. We can learn to become effective helpers with success rates ranging upwards from two-thirds to over 90 percent, against a base success rate of around 20 percent. Most importantly, we can use these skills to help ourselves and others to become healthy human beings and to form healthy human relationships.

THE FUTURE OF HELPING

The future of helping lies in systematic approaches to human resource development (HRD). Operating proactively, we may develop guidance and preventative mental health programs emphasizing youth resource development. Operating reactively, we may develop counseling, therapeutic and rehabilitation programs which programmatically move from the helpees' frames of reference to observable and measurable physical, emotional and intellectual development. The key is helping skills—helping skills which facilitate the helpees' movement through processing— exploring, understanding, acting. These helping skills emphasize interpersonal processing skills:

- Attending to involve the helpees
- Responding to facilitate helpee exploring
- Personalizing to facilitate helpee understanding
- Initiating to facilitate helpee acting.

What lies ahead are the information processing skills— thinking skills—required by the Age of Information in which we live. (Carkhuff, 1986, 1987)

APPENDIX C

REFERENCES

Adler, A. *Understanding Human Nature.* NY: Wolfe & Greenberg Publishers, 1927.

Anthony, W.A. A methodological investigation of the "minimally facilitative level of interpersonal function." *Journal of Clinical Psychology,* 1971, 27, 156–57.

Anthony, W.A. *The Principles of Psychiatric Rehabilitation.* Baltimore, MD: University Park Press, 1979.

Aspy, D.N., and Roebuck, F.N. An investigation of the relationship between levels of cognitive functioning and the teacher's classroom behavior. *Journal of Educational Research,* May, 1972.

Aspy, D.N., and Roebuck, F.N. *KIDS Don't Learn From People They Don't Like.* Amherst, MA: Human Resource Development Press, 1977.

Authier, J. Gustafson, K., Guerney, B., and Kasdorf, J.A. The psychological practitioner as a teacher. *Counseling Psychologist,* 1975, 5, 31–50.

Bandler, R., and Grinder, J. *The Structure of Magic I & II.* Palo Alto, CA: Science and Behavior Books, 1975.

Bandler, R., and Grinder, J. *Patterns of the Hypnotic Techniques of Milton H. Erickson, M.D.I.* Cupertino, CA: Meta Publications, 1975.

Barker, L.L. *Listening Behavior.* Englewood Cliffs, NJ: Prentice-Hall, 1971.

Berenson, B.G., and Carkhuff, R.R. *Sources of Gain in Counseling and Psychotherapy.* NY: Holt, Rinehart & Winston, 1967.

Berenson, B.G., and Mitchell, K.M. *Confrontation: For Better or Worse.* Amherst, MA.: Human Resource Development Press, 1974.

Berenson, D.H. The effects of systematic human relations training upon the classroom performance of elementary school teachers. *Journal of Research and Development in Education,* 1971, 4, 70–85.

Bergin, A.E., and Garfield, S.L. (Eds.). *Handbook of Psychotherapy and Behavioral Change.* NY: John Wiley & Sons, 1971.

Binswanger, L. Existential analysis and psychotherapy. In F. Fromm-Reichmann and J.L. Moreno (Eds.), *Progress in Psychotherapy.* NY: Grune & Stratton, 1956.

Birdwhistell, R. Some body motion elements accompanying spoken American English. In L. Thayter (Ed.), *Communication: Concepts and Perspectives.* Washington, DC: Spartan, 1967.

Brammer, L. *The Helping Relationship. 2nd ed.* Englewood Cliffs, NJ: Prentice-Hall, 1979.

Carkhuff, R.R. *Helping and Human Relations, Volumes I & II.* Amherst, MA: Human Resource Development Press, 1983 (a). NY: Holt, Rinehart & Winston, 1969.

Carkhuff, R.R. *The Development of Human Resources.* Amherst, MA: Human Resource Development Press, 1983 (b). NY: Holt, Rinehart & Winston, 1971 (a).

Carkhuff, R.R. Training as a preferred mode of treatment. *Journal of Counseling Psychology,* 1971 (b), 18, 123–131.

Carkhuff, R.R. *Cry Twice.* Amherst, MA: Human Resource Development Press, 1974.

Carkhuff, R.R. *Toward Actualizing Human Potential.* Amherst, MA: Human Resource Development Press, 1981.

Carkhuff, R.R. Interpersonal Skills and Human Productivity. Amherst, MA: Human Resource Development Press, 1983.

Carkhuff, R.R. *Productive Problem-Solving.* Amherst, MA: Human Resource Development Press, 1985 (a).

Carkhuff, R.R. *Productive Program Development.* Amherst, MA: Human Resource Development Press, 1985 (b).

Carkhuff, R.R. *Human Processing and Human Productivity.* Amherst, MA: Human Resource Development Press, 1986.

Carkhuff, R.R. *Learning and Thinking in the Age of Information.* Amherst, MA: Carkhuff Institute of Human Technology, 1987 (In Press).

Carkhuff, R.R., and Alexik, M. The effects of the manipulation of client depth of self-exploration upon high and low functioning counselors. *Journal of Clinical Psychology,* 1967, 23, 210–212.

Carkhuff, R.R., and Anthony, W.A. *The Skills of Helping.* Amherst, MA: Human Resource Development Press, 1979.

Carkhuff, R.R., and Becker, J. *Toward Excellence in Education.* Amherst, MA: Carkhuff Institute of Human Technology, 1979.

Carkhuff, R.R., and Berenson, B.G. *Beyond Counseling and Therapy.* NY: Holt, Rinehart & Winston, 1967, 1977.

Carkhuff, R.R., and Berenson, B.G. *Teaching as Treatment.* Amherst, MA: Human Resource Development Press, 1976.

Carkhuff, R.R., and Bierman, R. Training as a preferred mode of treatment of parents of emotionally disturbed children. *Journal of Counseling Psychology.* 1970, 17, 157–161.

Carkhuff, R.R., and Pierce, R.M. *Helping Begins at Home,* Amherst, MA: Human Resource Development Press, 1976.

Collingwood, T. HRD model and physical fitness. In D.W. Kratochvil (Ed.), *HRD Model in Education.* Baton Rouge, LA: Southern Universtiy, 1972.

Collingwood, T., Douds, A., Williams, H., and Wilson, R. *Developing Youth Resources,* Amherst, MA: Carkhuff Institute of Human Technology, 1978.

Combs, A., Avila D., and Purkey, W. *Helping Relationships: Basic Concepts for the Helping Professions.* Boston, MA: Allyn and Bacon, 1978.

Danish, S., and Hauer, A. *Helping Skills: A Basic Training Program.* NY: Behavioral Publications, 1973.

254

Egan, G. *The Skilled Helper.* Monterey, CA: Brooks, Cole, 1975.

Ekman, P., Friesen, W., and Ellworth, P. *Emotion in the Human Face.* NY: Pergammon, 1972.

Eysenck, H.J. The effects of psychotherapy. In H.J. Eysenck (Ed.), *The Handbook of Abnormal Psychology.* NY: Basic books, 1960.

Eysenck, H.J. The effects of psychotherapy. *International Journal of Psychotherapy,* 1965, 1, 99–178.

Freud, S. *New Introductory Lectures.* NY: Norton, 1933.

Fromm, E. *Man for Himself.* NY: Holt, Rinehart & Winston, 1947.

Garfield, S. Research on client variables in psychotherapy. In A.E. Bergin and S.L. Garfield (Eds.), *Handbook of Psychotherapy and Behavioral Change.* NY: Wiley & Sons, 1971.

Gazda, G. *Human Relations Development.* Boston, MA: Allyn and Bacon, 1973.

Genther, R., and Moughan, J. Introverts' and extroverts' responses to non-verbal attending behavior. *Journal of Counseling Psychology,* 1977, 24, 144–146.

Genther, R., and Saccuzzo, D. Accuracy of perceptions of psychotherapeutic content as a function of observers' levels of facilitation. *Journal of Clinical Psychology,* 1977, 33, 517–519.

Ginzberg, E., Ginsburg, S.W., Axelrod, S., and Herma, J.L. *Occupational Choice.* NY: Columbia University Press, 1951.

Goldstein, A., Sprafkin, R., and Gershaw, N. *Skill Training for Community Living.* NY: Pergammon Press, 1976.

Gordon, R. *Interviewing: Strategy, Techniques and Tactics.* Homewood, IL: Dorsey Press, 1975.

Hackney, H., and Cornier, L. *Counseling Strategies and Objectives.* 2nd ed. Englewood Cliffs, NJ: Prentice-Hall, 1979.

Hall, E. *The Silent Language.* NY: Doubleday, 1959.

Hall, E. *Beyond Culture.* NY: Doubleday, 1976.

Hefele, T.J. The effects of systematic human relations training upon student achievement. *Journal of Research and
Development in Education,* 1971, 4, 52–69.

Heidegger, M. *Being and Time.* London: SCM Press, 1962.

Holder, T., Carkhuff, R.R., and Berenson, B.G. The differential effects of the manipulation of therapeutic conditions
upon high and low functioning clients. *Journal of Counseling Psychology,* 1967, 14, 63–66.

Horney, K. *Our Inner Conflicts.* NY: Norton, 1945.

Ivey, A. The counselor as teacher. *Personnel and Guidance
Journal,* 1976, 54, 431–434.

Ivey, A., and Authier, J. *Microcounseling.* Springfield, IL:
Thomas, 1971, 1978.

Johnson, D. *Reaching Out: Interpersonal Effectiveness and
Self-Actualization.* Englewood Cliffs, NJ: Prentice-Hall,
1972.

Jung, C. *The Integration of the Personality.* NY: Holt, Rinehart
& Winston, 1939.

Krasner, L., and Ullman, L. *Research in Behavior Modification.* NY: Holt, Rinehart & Winston, 1965.

Levitt, E.E. Psychotherapy with children: A further evaluation.
Behavior Research and Therapy, 1963, 1, 45–51.

Lewis, W.W. Continuity and intervention in emotional disturb-
ance: A review. *Exceptional Children,* 1965, 31, 465–475.

May, R. (Ed.). *Existential Psychology.* NY: Random House,
1961.

Mehrabian, A. *Nonverbal Communication.* NY: Aldine-
Atherton, 1972.

Mickelson, D.J., and Stevic, R.R. Differential effects of
facilitative and non-facilitative behavioral counselors. *Journal of Counseling Psychology,* 1971, 18, 314–319.

256

Montgomery, C., and Brown, A. *In the Land of the Blind.* Amherst, MA: Carkhuff Institute of Human Technology, 1980.

Okun, B. *Effective Helping: Interviewing and Counseling Techniques.* North Scituate, MA: Duxbury Press, 1976.

Pagell, W., Carkhuff, R.R., and Berenson, B.G. The predicted differential effects of the level of counselor functioning upon the level of functioning of out-patients. *Journal of Clinical Psychology,* 1967, 23, 510–512.

Parsons, F. *Choosing a Vocation.* Boston, MA: Houghton Mifflin, 1909.

Patterson, C. *Theories of Counseling and Psychotherapy. 2nd ed.* NY: Harper & Row, 1973.

Piaget, G., Carkhuff, R.R., and Berenson, B.G. The development of skills in interpersonal functioning. *Counselor Education and Supervision,* 1968, 2, 102–106.

Pierce, R.M. and Drasgow, J. Teaching facilitative interpersonal functioning to psychiatric inpatients. *Journal of Counseling Psychology,* 1969, 16, 295–298.

Rank, O. *The Trauma of Birth.* NY: Harcourt, 1929.

Rogers, C., Gendlin, E., Keisler, D., and Truax, C. *The Therapeutic Relationship and Its Impact.* Westport (: Greenwood Press, 1967.

Schefflen, A. *Stream and Structure of Communication Behavior.* Bloomington, IN: Purdue University Press, 1969.

Smith-Hanen, S. Nonverbal behavior and counselor warmth and empathy. *Journal of Counseling Psychology,* 1977, 24, 84–91.

Sprinthall, N., and Mosher, R. Psychological education: A means to promote personal development during adolescence. *The Counseling Psychologist,* 1971, 2(4), 3–84.

Sullivan, H. The meaning of anxiety in psychiatry and life. *Psychiatry,* 1948, 11(1).

Super, D.E. *Appraising Vocational Fitness.* NY: Harper & Row, 1949.

Truax, C.B., and Carkhuff, R.R. *Toward Effective Counseling and Psychotherapy.* Chicago, IL: Aldine, 1967.

Vitalo, R. The effects of facilitative interpersonal functioning in a conditioning paradigm. *Journal of Counseling Psychology,* 1970, 17, 141–144.

Watson, J.B. Behaviorism and the concept of mental disease. *Journal of Philosophical Psychology,* 1916, 13, 589–597.

Wolpe, J., Salter, A., and Renya, L. *The Conditioning Therapies.* NY: Holt, Rinehart & Winston, 1964.

259

APPENDIX D

ANNOTATED BIBLIOGRAPHY

Recent Research and Models

Carkhuff, R.R.
Learning and Thinking in the Age of Information
Amherst, MA: Carkhuff Institute of Human Technology,
1987 (in press).
Critical for helpers and educators who wish to understand information processing skills. Surveys the
literature and models of learning. Distinguishes between conditioning, learning and thinking. Teaches
learning and thinking skills.

Carkhuff, R.R.
Human Processing and Human Productivity
Amherst, MA: Human Resource Development Press, 1986.
Provides an empirical base for the prepotency human—
information processing in the Age of Information. Establishes that 85% of the variability in economic productivity growth is accounted for by human and information
resource development. Posits individual, interpersonal
and organizational processing as the effective ingredients of human processing and human productivity.

Carkhuff, R.R.
*The Exemplar—The Exemplary Performer in the Age of
Information*
Amherst, MA: Human Resource Development Press, 1984.
Distinguishes movement from the Industrial through the
Electronics to the Information Age. Establishes human
processing as the critical ingredient in human perfor-
mance. Provides performance models for developing
exemplary performance.

Carkhuff, R.R.
Sources of Human Productivity
Amherst, MA: Human Resource Development Press, 1983.
Useful for professionals in private as well as public sector
agencies. Provides empirical base and models for re-
lating human technology to human resource development

and individual performance and, thus, organizational productivity. Describes policy-making, management, supervision and delivery functions and skills for human and educational service agencies as well as business and government.

Carkhuff, R.R.
Interpersonal Skills and Human Productivity
Amherst, MA: Human Resource Development Press, 1983. Useful for professionals in private as well as public sector agencies. Summarizes two decades of research of interpersonal skills in 164 studies of 158,884 recipients. Describes the effects of helper interpersonal skills as well as direct training of helpees upon outcome indices of helpee functioning in living, learning and working.

Carkhuff, R.R.
Toward Actualizing Human Potential
Amherst, MA: Human Resource Development Press, 1981. Useful for understanding the critical dimensions of Human Resource Development. Presents methods of measuring the physical, emotional, and intellectual dimensions of human potential.

Research and Models

Aspy, D.N.
This is School! Sit Down and Listen!
Amherst, MA: Human Resource Development Press, 1986. Summarizes research of over 200,000 hours of classroom teaching. Aspy summarizes his findings in the titles of his chapters:
- *Don't Feel!*
- *Don't Think!*
- *Don't Talk*
- *Line Up!*
- *Don't Get Involved!*

Aspy, D.N. and Roebuck, F.N.
Kids Don't Learn from People They Don't Like
Amherst, MA: Human Resource Development Press, 1977.
Useful for understanding the research base for the Carkhuff Model in teaching. Hundreds of teachers were trained in interpersonal skills. The effects on thousands of
learners were studied. Significant gains were achieved on
the following indices: student absenteeism and tardiness;
student discipline and school crises; student learning
skills and cognitive growth. Concludes that the Carkhuff
Model is the preferred teacher training model.

Berenson, B.G.
*Belly-to-Belly and Back-to-Back: The Militant Humanism of
Robert R. Carkhuff*
Amherst, MA: Human Resource Development Press, 1975.
Useful for an understanding of the human assumptions
underlying the human resource development models of
Carkhuff. Presents a collection of prose and poetry by
Carkhuff. Concludes by challenging us to die growing.

Berenson, B.G. and Carkhuff, R.R.
The Sources of Gain in Counseling and Psychotherapy
NY: Holt, Rinehart & Winston, 1967.
Useful for an in-depth view of the different orientations
to helping. Integrates the research of diverse approaches to helping. Concludes with a model of core
conditions around which the different preferred modes
of treatment make their own unique contributions to
helpee benefits.

Berenson, B.G. and Mitchell, K.M.
Confrontation: For Better or Worse
Amherst, MA: Human Resource Development Press, 1974.
Useful for an in-depth view of confrontation and immediacy as well as the core interpersonal dimensions.
Presents extensive experimental manipulation of core
interpersonal skills and confrontation and immediacy.
Concludes that while confrontation is never necessary
and never sufficient, in the hands of an effective helper,
it may be efficient for moving the helpee toward constructive gain or change.

Carkhuff, R.R.
*Helping and Human Relations. Vol. I Selection and Train-
ing. Vol II Practice and Research*
Amherst, MA: Human Resource Development Press, 1983.
NY: Holt, Rinehart & Winston, 1969.
Useful for understanding the research base for interpersonal skills in counseling and education. Operationalizes the helping process in great detail. Presents extensive research evidence for systematic selection, training
and treatment procedures. Concludes that teaching is
the preferred mode of treatment for helping.

Carkhuff, R.R.
The Development of Human Resources
Amherts, MA: Human Resource Development Press, 1983.
NY: Holt, Rinehart & Winston, 1971.
Useful for understanding applications of human
resource development (HRD) models. Describes and
presents research evidence for numerous applications
of helping skills training in human, educational and
community resource development. Concludes that systematic planning for human delivery systems can be effectively translated into human benefits.

Carkhuff, R.R., Devine, J., Berenson, B.G., Griffin, A.H.,
Angelone, R., Keeling, T., Patch, W. and Steinberg, H.
Cry Twice!
Amherst, MA: Human Resource Development Press, 1974.
Useful for understanding the ingredients of institutional
change. Details the people, programs and organizational variables needed to transform an institution from
a custodial to a treatment orientation. Concludes that
institutional change begins with people change.

Collingwood, T., Douds, A., Williams, H., and Wilson, R.D.
Developing Youth Resources Through Police Diversion
Amherst, MA: Carkhuff Institute of Human Technology, 1978.
Useful for understanding the effective ingredients of
delinquency prevention and youth rehabilitation. The
purpose of the program described was to provide services at the police level to juvenile offenders in order to
reduce recidivism by delivering skills training and by
monitoring services to youth and parents. Concludes
that with systematic skills training programs, with skilled
personnel, and with an organizational framework in a
police department, you can make a dramatic and constructive impact on juvenile offender recidivism.

Carkhuff, R.R. and Berenson, B.G.
Beyond Counseling and Therapy
NY: Holt, Rinehart & Winston, Second Edition, 1977.
Useful for understanding of the core interpersonal conditions and their implications and applications. Adds
many core dimensions and factors them out as responsive and initiative dimensions. Includes an analysis of
the client-centered, existential, psychoanalytic, trait-and-
factor and behavioristic orientations to counseling and
psychotherapy. Concludes that only the trait-and-factor
and behavioristic positions make unique contributions to
human benefits over and above the core conditions.

Carkhuff, R.R. and Berenson, B.G.
Teaching as Treatment
Amherst, MA: Human Resource Development Press, 1976.
Useful for understanding the development of a human
technology. Operationalizes the helping process as
teaching. Offers research evidence for living, learning
and working skills development and physical, emotional
and intellectual outcomes. Concludes that learning-to-
learn is the fundamental model for living, learning and
working.

Truax, C.B. and Carkhuff, R.R.
Toward Effective Counseling and Therapy
Chicago: Aldine, 1967.
   Useful for understanding the transitional phases in developing helping models. Presents extensive evidence on training lay and professional helpers as well as different orientations to helping. Concludes that the core interpersonal dimensions of empathy, respect and genuineness are critical to effective helping.

Skills Development and Applications

LIVING SKILLS

Carkhuff, R.R.
The Art of Helping VI—Trainer's Guide
Amherst, MA: Human Resource Development Press, 1987.
   Useful training techniques for teaching helpers. Includes attending, responding, personalizing and initiating learning exercises with counseling applications.

Carkhuff, R.R., et al.
The Art of Helping VI—Student Workbook
Amherst, MA: Human Resource Development Press, 1987.
   Useful for bridging the gap between reading about helping skills in the text and practicing the skills in training sessions. Includes practice exercises for attending, responding, personalizing and initiating skills.

Carkhuff, R.R.
Productive Problem-Solving
Amherst, MA: Human Resource Development, Press, 1985.
   Useful for developing decision-making skills. Includes modules on defining problems and goals and selecting and implementing courses of action.

Carkhuff, R.R.
Productive Program Development
Amherst, MA: Human Resource Development Press, 1985.
   Useful for developing program development skills. Includes modules on defining goals and developing and implementing programs to achieve the goals.

Carkhuff, R.R., et al.

The Art of Helping Video Series

Amherst, MA: Human Resources Development Press, 1986.

Featuring Dr. Robert R. Carkhuff, this series is designed to skill practitioners and students in counseling techniques by demonstrating helping skills in real life interactions.

Tape #1—*Helping Overview*

Dr. Carkhuff interacts with a teacher and students on the evolution and future of helping. 24 minutes

Tape #2—*Attending Skills*

Dr. Carkhuff supervising students who are learning helping skills in attending physically, observing, and listening. 23 minutes

Tape #3—*Responding Skills*

Dr. Carkhuff supervising students who are learning helping skills in responding to content, feeling, and meaning. 18 minutes

Tape #4—*Personalizing Skills*

Dr. Carkhuff supervising students who are learning helping skills in personalizing meaning, problems, and goals. 17 minutes

Tape #5—*Initiating Skills*

Dr. Carkhuff supervising students who are learning initiating skills in defining goals and developing programs. 17 minutes

Tape #6—*Helping Colleen*

Dr. Carkhuff helps a young woman to deal with professional and personal role conflicts. 22 minutes

Tape #7—*Helping Tyrone*

Dr. Carkhuff helps a young man to understand his enormous resources in making critical personal and career decisions in his life. 18 minutes

Tape #8—*Helping Gil*
Dr. Carkhuff helps a recovering alcoholic deal with his
fear of failing others and regressing himself. 29 minutes

Tape #9—*Helping Rose*
Dr. Bernard Berenson helps the mother of a young
child as she deals with a conflict of emotional and intellectual values. 30 minutes

Carkhuff, R.R. and Anthony, W.A.
The Skills of Helping
Amherst, MA: Human Resource Development Press, 1979.
Useful for training helpers in helping skills. Includes at-
tending, responding, personalizing, problem-solving,
program development and initiating skills.

TEACHING SKILLS

Carkhuff, R.R.
The Productive Teacher Vol. I—Curriculum Development
Vol. II—Instruction
Amherst, MA: Human Resource Development Press, 1984.
Presents innovative models for the critical skills of curriculum development and instruction: defining learning
objectives; developing skills content; developing
teaching delivery plans; delivering content; relating to
learners' frames of reference to the content.

Carkhuff, R.R. and Fisher, S.
*Instructional Systems Design. Vol. I—Designing the Instruc-
tional System. Vol. II—Evaluating the Instructional System*
Amherst, MA: Human Resource Development Press, 1984.
Presents innovative models for the critical skills of instructional systems design and evaluation: establishing
goals; analyzing tasks; defining skills objectives;
developing skills content; developing delivery plans;
making the delivery; evaluating the processing, acquisi-
tion, application and transfer of skills and the achievement of goals.

Carkhuff, R.R., Berenson, D.H. and Pierce, R.M.
  The Skills of Teaching: Interpersonal Skills
  Amherst, MA: Human Resource Development Press, 1977.
    Useful for preservice and inservice teachers. Includes
    attending, responding, personalizing and initiating
    modules with classroom applications.

Carkhuff, R.R. and Pierce, R.M.
  Training Delivery Skills. Vol. I—Planning the Delivery
  Vol. II—Making the Delivery
  Amherst, MA: Human Resource Development Press, 1984.
    Presents innovative models for the critical skills of plan-
    ning and making the delivery and defining objectives;
    developing content; developing plans; making the train-
    ing delivery.

The Carkhuff Institute of Human Technology
  The Skills of Teaching Video Series
  Amherst, MA: Carkhuff Institute of Human Technology, 1986.
    Video-based training programs derived from over
    200,000 hours of classroom research. Each unit con-
    sists of a videotape, participant's skillbook, and trainer's
    guide. Based on the work of Drs. David Aspy, Cheryl
    Aspy, Bernard Berenson, David Berenson, Robert R.
    Carkhuff, Ned Flanders, Andrew Griffin, and Flora
    Roebuck. Useful for preservice and inservice teacher
    training.

  Tape #1—*Interpersonal Skills for Teachers*
    This module helps teachers learn the interpersonal
    skills for facilitating student involvement. Based upon
    the Carkhuff model for interpersonal skills. 17 minutes

  Tape #2—*The ROPES of Lesson-Planning*
    This instructional module teaches the *ROPES* method
    of lesson-planning developed by Carkhuff and Dr. David
    Berenson. Teachers who use this method spend less
    time lecturing and are able to help their students im-
    merse themselves more fully in learning. 20 minutes

Tape #3—*The LEAST Method of Discipline*
An instructional module on an effective discipline management tool. Developed by Dr. Carkhuff and Dr. Andrew H. Griffin and field-tested on hundreds of thousands of teachers, this module will give teachers the ability to discipline constructively, not destructively. 24 minutes

Tape #4—*Assessing Classroom Cognitive Functioning*
Based on Dr. David Aspy's adaptation of Dr. Bloom's *Taxonomy of Educational Objectives*, this module provides practical methods for measuring cognitive functioning. 19 minutes

Tape #5—*Assessing Teacher-Student Interactions*
An instructional module in facilitating effective teacher-student interactions. Based upon Dr. Flanders' *Interaction Analysis* and extensive research by Drs. Aspy and Flora Roebuck. Features Drs. Aspy and Flanders. 25 minutes

Tape #6—*This is School*
A presentation by Dr. Aspy on his conclusions from over 200,000 hours of classroom research. Research from all levels of education, early childhood through graduate and post-graduate. 20 minutes

Tape #7—*The Black Experience*
Dr. Andrew H. Griffin as interviewed by Dr. Bernard Berenson. An inspired perspective on the educational experience of blacks in America today. 30 minutes

WORKING SKILLS

Carkhuff, R.R. and Friel, T.W.
The Art of Developing a Career—Student's Guide
Amherst, MA: Human Resource Development Press, 1974.
Useful for developing careers. Includes modules on ex-
panding, narrowing and planning for career alternatives.

Carkhuff, R.R., Pierce, R.M., Friel, T.W. and Willis, D.
GETAJOB
Amherst, MA: Human Resource Development Press, 1975.
Useful for developing placement skills. Includes
modules on finding jobs, preparing resumes and hand-
ling job interviews.

Friel, T.W. and Carkhuff, R.R.
The Art of Developing a Career—Helper's Guide
Amherst, MA: Human Resource Development Press, 1974.
Useful training skills for helpers and teachers. Includes
methods for involving the learners in exploring,
understanding and acting upon their careers.

FITNESS SKILLS

Collingwood, T. and Carkhuff, R.R.
Get Fit for Living
Amherst, MA: Human Resource Development Press, 1976.
Useful for developing physical fitness. Includes modules
for self-assessing, setting goals and developing and im-
plementing fitness programs.

Collingwood, T. and Carkhuff, R.R.
Get Fit for Living—Trainer's Guide
Amherst, MA: Human Resource Development Press, 1976.
Useful training skills for fitness trainers. Includes
methods and programs for delivering fitness skills.

APPLICATIONS

Anthony, W.A. and Carkhuff, R.R.
The Art of Health Care
Amherst, MA: Human Resource Development Press, 1976.
Useful for health care workers. Includes modules and
applications of interpersonal, decision-making and pro-
gram development skills in health care facilities.

Carkhuff, R.R.
Productive Parenting Skills
Amherst, MA: Human Resource Development Press, 1985.
Presents innovative models for the critical skills (attending, responding, personalizing, initiating) and content
(helping, teaching, working, community development) of
parenting.

Carkhuff, R.R. and Pierce, R.M.
Teacher as Person
Washington, DC: National Education Association, 1976.
Useful for teachers interested in multi-cultural educa-
tion. Includes modules and applications of interpersonal
skills in the school.

Carkhuff, R.R. and Pierce, R.M.
Helping Begins at Home
Amherst, MA: Human Resource Development Press, 1976.
Useful for parents interested in parenting skills. In-
cludes modules and applications of interpersonal and
program development skills in the home.

Scott, Sharon
Peer Pressure Reversal
Amherst, MA: Human Resource Development Press, 1985.
Presents the critical skills for reversing peer pressure:
1. Checking out the scene
2. Make a good decision
3. Act to avoid trouble

Index